Slam Dunk

Slam Dunk

Kate Jaimet

orca sports

ORCA BOOK PUBLISHERS

Library and Archives Canada Cataloguing in Publication

Jaimet, Kate, 1969-
Slam dunk / written by Kate Jaimet.

(Orca sports)
ISBN 978-1-55469-132-6 (pbk.)
ISBN 978-1-55469-162-3 (bound)

I. Title. II. Series.
PS8619.A368S53 2009   jC813'.6   C2008-907418-1

Summary: When his star point guard goes missing, sixteen-year-old
Slam Amaro finds out that coaching a girls' high school
basketball team isn't the slam dunk he thought it would be.

First published in the United States, 2009
Library of Congress Control Number: 2008941141

Orca Book Publishers gratefully acknowledges the support for its publishing
programs provided by the following agencies: the Government of Canada
through the Book Publishing Industry Development Program and the
Canada Council for the Arts, and the Province of British Columbia through
the BC Arts Council and the Book Publishing Tax Credit.

Cover design by Teresa Bubela
Cover photography by Getty Images
Author photo by Mark Purves

Orca Book Publishers
PO Box 5626, Stn. B
Victoria, BC Canada
V8R 6S4

Orca Book Publishers
PO Box 468
Custer, WA USA
98240-0468

www.orcabook.com
Printed and bound in Canada.
Printed on 100% PCW recycled paper.
12 11 10 09 • 4 3 2 1

chapter one

I knew the team was in trouble when our star point guard showed up to the game with a black eye. It wasn't just a shiner either. Inez's left cheek was black and green. Her eye was so swollen she could barely see out of it. Inez wouldn't say who'd hit her, just that it was an accident during a "friendly game" over the weekend. Man, friends like that we didn't need. Especially going into our last regular-season game against the top-ranked Glebe Gryphons, the only team ahead of us in the standings.

The trouble started with the first whistle. Ifrah, our six-foot center, won the jump and tapped the ball back. The ball flew toward Inez in a smooth arc. It should have been an easy catch to set up our first offensive play. But Inez let the ball slip through her fingers. Before she could turn and catch it, a Glebe player dashed past her, grabbed the ball on the bounce and charged down the court. Breakaway. Layup. Basket. Score: 2–0. Time: five seconds into the first quarter. It was going to be a long game.

Here's the thing: If I were the coach, I never would have let Inez start in the first place. Put her on the injury roster. Nothing wrong with that. Why get her morale down in the last game before the playoffs? But, hey, I was just the assistant coach. Besides, the coach was Inez's mom. I wasn't going to get involved in *that*. So I kept my mouth shut and marked the two points on my stats sheet.

I know what you're thinking: a guy's got better things to do with his time than volunteer as assistant coach of a chicks' high school basketball team. But trust me, I've got a good reason.

See, I'm trying out for the Ontario Under 17 basketball team. The team that represents the province at the Canada-wide championships. The next step is the Ontario Under 19 team, then the Canadian national team and then the Olympics. It's all part of my plan.

When you try out for the Ontario team, they make you fill in this form with all your experience and your marks in school and stuff. Then there's this space for "community activities." Man, my only "community activity" is hanging out at the park shooting hoops. So when Mrs. Ramirez asked me if I wanted to be her assistant coach for the Brookfield Blues girls' team, I said, "Sure." I said it with a shrug, you know, because I didn't want to look too keen about coaching a bunch of chicks. But secretly I was thinking, if it helps me make the provincial team, I'm all over it like a tensor bandage on a bad knee.

Mrs. Ramirez is a phys-ed teacher, or at least she was back in Chile. Here, she's a substitute teacher, plus she comes in on Mondays to teach our Spanish class.

Seeing as how Mrs. Ramirez is Inez's mom, I could understand why it was hard for her to bench Inez. But Inez really needed to be benched. She was a dribbling disaster out there.

The first half dragged on and on. All I could do was record the wreckage on my stats sheet. With one minute left to go in the first half, we'd given away twelve interceptions and got nailed six times for three-in-the-key. Inez hadn't scored once. It was 34–20. I was just praying it wouldn't get any worse before the buzzer sounded. Praying for it to get better would have been asking too much.

Inez had the ball at the top of the key. The other players were running cuts to shake off their defenders. Then we caught a lucky break. Ifrah's defender stumbled. Ifrah sprinted into the key. She called for the ball. But Inez, at the right top corner of the key, couldn't see Ifrah, who was down to the left. Inez swiveled around to see out of her good right eye. In that movement, she exposed the ball to the Glebe player guarding her.

It only took a split second. With one flick of her hand, the Glebe girl swiped the ball away and took off down the court. Inez ran after her, but she was already three strides behind. The Glebe girl pounded down the court as the clock ticked down. Five seconds, four seconds, three seconds, two seconds, a jump shot from the top of the key. Swoosh. The buzzer sounded just as the ball hit the floor. End of the first half, and we were trailing by sixteen points.

I grabbed the caddy of water bottles and a pile of towels, along with my stats sheets, and followed the team as they trudged into the locker room.

The locker room was clammy and smelled like girls' sweat, which is kind of pungent, but not as bad as guys' sweat, which is really rank. I passed around the water bottles and listened to the girls gripe about the game.

"Number 20 fouled me!"

"She plays dirty!"

"And the ref's not calling anything!"

It's like that when your team's behind. Everybody blames the ref. The chicks were no different, except for Inez. She just slumped down in a corner and didn't say anything.

I went over to give her a water bottle personally. You know, just because I felt bad for her. I mean, if you've got a black eye and you can't see anything, it's not your fault your team's losing. I was going to say something like that to her, but she didn't even look up at me. Just took the water bottle and mumbled, "Thanks, Slam." So I left her alone and went back to the girls clustered around Mrs. Ramirez.

"Okay, Maddy." Mrs. Ramirez turned to the second-string point guard. "You'll be going in for Inez. That means we're going to change our strategy a little bit."

On her clipboard, Mrs. Ramirez started showing the girls the play she wanted them to run. I didn't pay much attention, because I'm not really a playbook kind of guy.

When I say that, I mean I'm more of a natural athlete. The way I see it, if you want to *be* good, you do what *feels* good. Because if it doesn't *feel* good, it's not going to *be* good, you know what I mean? You've got to get into the Zone. Once you get into the Zone, good things start to happen. That's what I was planning to do for the provincial tryouts on the weekend. Just get into the Zone, you know?

Inez was the kind of player who did that for her team. When she was on her game, the girls really got into the Zone. But right now, they didn't have that going. They didn't have anything going at all.

Mrs. Ramirez looked at her watch.

"Okay, girls, let's put the first half behind us. We're going to be meeting these guys again in the playoffs, so I want you to go out there and show them your stuff."

The girls huddled together and gave their cheer, "Goooooo Blues!" Then they filed out of the locker room. All except Inez. She was still sitting hunched over in the corner. She'd taken her long brown hair out of its ponytail, so it was hanging down, hiding her face.

Mrs. Ramirez looked at Inez. Then she turned around and handed me her clipboard.

"Salvador, get out there and coach the second half."

"But..."

"Just do it," she said. Then she went to sit beside her daughter. She put her arm around Inez's shoulders.

I'm not a violent guy, but at that moment I felt like throwing a punch at whoever had given Inez that black eye. Why wouldn't she tell anyone who did it?

I headed for the change-room door, but couldn't stop myself from taking one quick look back at Inez before I went out. Thing was, I could hear a kind of sniffling from the corner where she was sitting. I didn't want to stare or anything, but it looked to me like Inez was crying.

chapter two

Salvador. Mrs. Ramirez is the only one apart from my parents who calls me that. Everyone else just calls me Slam. Get it? Salvador Luis **Am**aro—Slam. Plus, I have this really sweet slam dunk that I've been working on for over a year. It goes like this: step right, dribble, step left, pick up the ball, plant my right foot and drive up with my left knee. I'm in the air. I pass the ball under my left knee, around my back, into my right hand, lift it high and slam!

Into the basket. Sweet. It's what I call my signature move.

Man, if that slam dunk didn't win me a spot on the provincial team, the coaches would have to be blind, I'm telling you, blind.

By the time I got to the bench, the ref was blowing his whistle to start the second half. I took a glance at Mrs. Ramirez's clipboard to see what the girls were supposed to be doing. Looked like a give-and-go play, which was fine with me. Like I said, I'm not really a playbook kind of guy, but if it helped the girls, great. I mean, they needed all the help they could get.

Ifrah took possession and passed the ball to Maddy, our second-string point guard. Maddy carried it down the court. She waited for the pick, passed the ball and made a dash down the side of the key. She got the give-and-go pass, pivoted and took a jump shot. Rebound off the rim.

Rebound. And what were our girls doing about it? Standing there gawking, that's what.

"Rebound! Get the rebound!" I jumped to my feet but it was too late. A Glebe girl leapt for the ball and grabbed it midair. She passed it out of the key and Glebe went to the offense.

Did we try for an interception? Did we try for a turnover in their end? No, we scooted back to our key to set up a zone defense. Which is fine if you're, like, ten points ahead. But we were sixteen points behind. In another two minutes, it was eighteen. Maddy took the throw-in, and I motioned for her to call for a time-out.

I know, three minutes into the quarter and I'm calling for a time-out. It doesn't look good. It looks like I'm panicking. But hey, Mrs. Ramirez told me to take over. And I wasn't going to get blown away by following her playbook. It was time for some Slam action.

"Okay, girls," I said as they made a circle around me. "I want full-court, man-to-man defense. I want you to stick to them like glue. Don't let them pass. Don't let them shoot. Don't even let them take it over center. Force the interception, okay? Force the turnaround. I want us to score six points before they even get into our end again. Got it? And Ifrah? Rebounds! I want you in there for the rebounds."

"Who's taking number 20?" one girl said.

Number 20 was a big-boned girl who used her butt as a weapon of attack. Elbows like jackhammers and a mouth like a gangsta rapper. I looked around for the toughest girl on our team. Brenda. Number 17. Brenda was a rugby player with buzz-cut black hair and a yin-and-yang tattoo on the back of her neck.

"Brenda, you're on number 20," I said.

"She plays dirty," Ifrah warned her.

"If she shoves you around, shove her right back," I said. Brenda nodded. The whistle blew, and the girls ran back on the court.

They ran the same give-and-go play on offense. This time, it worked. A clean jump shot and two points. Glebe got the throw-in, but they couldn't do anything with it. Our girls were hanging onto them like prom dates on the senior football team.

Finally the Glebe forward tried to lob a throw-in, but Ifrah intercepted it. Layup, two points. It went on like that for a couple of plays. Before Glebe could get the ball into our end, we'd scored eight points. Not six, but eight. So we were only trailing by ten points. I know, ten points is still a big lead, but I had this feeling the girls were in their Zone now. I always say, you've got to believe in the Zone.

By the last minute of the third quarter, we'd clawed the lead down to eight points. The Glebe girls were starting to get mad, especially number 20, who couldn't shake Brenda no matter how hard she tried. There were forty seconds left in the third quarter. I was thinking if we could score one more basket before the buzzer, we'd get the momentum going into the last quarter and we'd have a good shot at winning. Not too shabby for Coach Slam's first game.

Glebe's point guard had the ball at the top of our key. She passed to number 20 way outside, but I wasn't worried. Number 20 couldn't jump shoot for beans. If she wanted to drive to the basket, she'd have to get around Brenda.

I couldn't believe what happened next. Number 20 put her head down and charged like a linebacker, hit Brenda with her shoulder and elbow and kept going straight for the basket.

"Foul!" I jumped up. "Hey, ref! Foul!"

Number 20 finished the layup. The ball swished through the net. The ref blew his whistle.

"Foul!" he called. "Foul on number 17, Brookfield."

Number 17, Brookfield? Foul on Brenda?

"Hey, ref!" I shouted. "What are you, blind? Are you crazy?"

The ref grabbed the ball and marched over to me. He was a short little dude with a mustache and a red face.

"What's your name, kid?" he said.

"I'm the coach," I straightened my shoulders and looked down at him.

"Oh, yeah? Where's your teacher-supervisor?"

"She's in the change room with an injured player. She put me in charge."

"Oh, yeah? Well, any more lip out of you, and it's a game suspension."

"Oh, yeah?" I said. I was just about to tell him what I thought of him and his lousy game suspension, when something made me shut my mouth.

The something was this: it wouldn't look too good if the coaches for the provincial team found out I got a game suspension for giving lip to a ref. So even though I knew I should stick up for the girls, I couldn't risk blowing my chance at getting on the provincial team.

I gave him my coolest shrug.

"Whatever," I said.

"Next time, keep it to yourself, kid," said the ref.

He marched down to our end, handed the ball to number 20, and she sank the free throw. You can bet that by the time the buzzer sounded for the end of the third quarter, our Brookfield girls were cranky and bummed out.

I don't know if you've ever been surrounded by a bunch of cranky, bummed-out girls, but it is not fun. Not fun at all.

"That ref's a jerk!"

"Number 20 plays dirty!"

"How long do we have to play this man-to-man defense? I'm wiped out!"

"Where's Inez?"

"Where's Mrs. Ramirez?"

"Okay, okay, girls!" I had to shout to get them to listen to me. Finally they calmed down and looked at me like maybe I had some brilliant strategy up my sleeve that would save the game. Suddenly I wished I'd paid a little more attention to playbooks and all that stuff. Not for me—like I said, I'm a naturally inspired player—but for the girls. All I could think of was to keep up the full-court press.

"Okay, girls, we're only twelve points behind. Six baskets. All we've got to do is keep up the pressure."

The girls groaned. Ifrah slumped to the bench.

"I can't. I'm beat. I need a sub."

"I can't sub you, Ifrah. I need you for the rebounds."

She looked at me like her Nike Airs had no air left in them.

"Come on you guys, we can win this game," I told them.

"I don't care if we win," growled Brenda. "I just want to take out number 20."

The ref blew his whistle, and the girls dragged themselves back onto the court, but their hearts weren't in it anymore. Ifrah could barely keep up with the girl she was supposed to be defending. That man-to-man, full-court press had taken it out of her.

I kept glancing back to the change-room door, but Inez and Mrs. Ramirez didn't come out. It was pretty clear they weren't going to miraculously save us from losing. After five minutes I subbed Ifrah and let the rest of the girls go back to the zone defense. After all, we were still going to make the playoffs. There was no point in killing the girls for a hopeless cause.

"Good game, Ifrah," I said as she flopped down on the bench.

"Thanks, Coach," she said.

Even though we were losing, that sounded sweet to my ears: "Thanks, Coach." I could definitely get used to that.

I'm not going to go into the gory details of how the fourth quarter went down. Let's just say they whupped us bad. Creamed us. Wiped the floor with us. Whatever you want to call it. It was pretty obvious that if Inez didn't get back on her game, we weren't going to be hoisting any championship trophy when we met Glebe again in the playoffs.

"Not your fault, Slam," said Ifrah, as the girls trudged into the change room. "You coming to Cinnamon's?"

Cinnamon's is a café around the corner where the girls go after games sometimes. I didn't really want to hang out with a bunch of bummed-out girls, especially after I'd just coached them to their season's biggest loss. But there are rules about belonging to a team. One of them is, you don't abandon your teammates when they're down.

"Yeah, sure," I said.

Ifrah turned to follow the other girls to the change room. I stopped her just before she went in.

"Hey, Ifrah," I said. "Could you check on Inez for me?"

"Okay."

Ifrah went into the change room and came out about half a minute later. She had this look on her face like something was really wrong. More wrong than just losing the game.

"Inez and her mom," she said. "They're gone."

chapter three

Gone? What was up with that? I mean, you don't just take off. Especially not if you're the coach and the star point guard. It was just weird.

When I caught up with the girls at Cinnamon's, that's all they were talking about.

"Does anyone have Inez's cell-phone number?" said Brenda. She was crammed into a booth with Ifrah and Maddy and a couple of the other girls. They were all drinking those girly frappa-cappa-whatevers.

"Are you kidding?" said Ifrah. "Her dad won't let her have a cell phone."

"Omigod, he's super strict," Maddy chimed in. "She was, like, freaking out on Saturday night because her bus was late and she was going to miss her curfew. Her dad was going to totally ground her. And we weren't even doing anything. We just went for a movie and a slice of pizza. There weren't any guys for, like, miles around."

"Miles?" said Ifrah.

"You know what I mean," Maddy rolled her eyes. "Like, no guys that we knew. I mean, we weren't *going out* with anyone."

"Anyway"—Ifrah slurped her drink—"her dad obviously didn't *totally* ground her, because she played basketball on Sunday morning."

"Yeah, and got that black eye." Maddy slumped back into the corner of the booth. "Maybe he *should* have grounded her."

I pulled up a chair, set it backward at the edge of the girls' booth and straddled the seat, cowboy-style. It's weird, sitting around with a bunch of girls. I mean, if it looks like all the girls are digging you, that's cool. But if it looks like you're a wuss, that's different. One thing you don't do is order a frappa-cappa-whatever with chocolate sprinkles on top. I dug around in my backpack and pulled out a bottle of Gatorade.

"I bet I know who gave Inez that black eye," Brenda said.

"Who?" Maddy gasped.

"You know that number 20 on the Glebe team? The one who fouled me in the third quarter? Well, she plays in that pickup game at the Y on Sunday mornings. The same game Inez plays in."

"No way!" said Maddy.

"Way," said Brenda. "And don't you think she'd love to take out our starting point guard just before the playoffs?"

"Totally," said Maddy. "We should do something about it."

"Hang on," Ifrah broke in. "Inez said it was an accident."

"Inez!" Brenda snorted. "Inez never says anything bad about anyone. You know that."

"Well, even if someone did it on purpose, you don't even have any proof it was that Glebe girl," said Ifrah.

"Proof! Omigod, Ifrah," said Maddy. "You are so *CSI*."

The girls laughed, but I didn't get the joke. That's the thing about hanging around with a bunch of girls. They know all kinds of stuff about each other that you don't know. It kind of makes you feel clueless.

"Ifrah wants to join the RCMP," Brenda explained.

"Correction: I'm *going* to join the RCMP," Ifrah said. "Besides, even if number 20 did give Inez a black eye, what are you going to do? Go punch her in the face for messing with our playoff chances?"

"It's not just about the playoffs, Ifrah," said Maddy, with this tone of accusation in her voice that shut Ifrah right up.

"Yeah, I know," said Ifrah. She looked down and stirred her frappa-thingy with a wooden coffee stick. Nobody else at the table said anything. I could tell I was missing something, again.

I shot a look at Brenda, and she filled me in.

"Inez wants to go to the basketball camp at Carleton U this summer. She needs to impress a scout so she can get a scholarship."

"Yeah, but she can go even without a scholarship," I said. The girls just looked at each other without saying anything and fidgeted with their drinks. I knew I'd said something stupid. The only question was, how stupid?

"Her parents can't afford to send her, Slam," Brenda said.

Oh. Real stupid.

"They only immigrated a few years ago. From Chile," Ifrah said.

I knew Mrs. Ramirez came from Chile, because she spoke Spanish with the same accent as my parents. My parents came to Canada a long time ago, in the 1980s. I figured Inez and her mom had come over at the same time, because my dad told me a lot of people left the country then.

Dad said there was this guy, Pinochet, running the government in Chile. If he didn't like someone, he made them disappear and they were never heard from again. Disappear, as in die. My parents were both law students, and they did a few things that put them on the government's bad side—protests and stuff. Then Dad's older brother "disappeared," so Dad and Mom decided to "disappear" to Canada, where this Pinochet guy couldn't get at them.

The girls were finishing up their drinks and getting ready to leave. I chugged the rest of my Gatorade and threw my backpack over my shoulder.

"I hope Inez is going to be okay," said Maddy.

"I'll message her on Facebook tonight," said Ifrah.

"You can't," said Brenda. "Her dad made her take down her Facebook account a couple weeks ago, remember?"

"I know." Ifrah got this wicked grin on her face. "She put up a new one. Under a fake name: Trixie Hoopster."

Trixie Hoopster. It was a cool fake name. I made a mental note to go on Facebook and sign up as her friend. 'Cause if Inez's dad was as strict as the girls said, he probably didn't like guys hanging around his daughter. And who knows? There might be a time when I'd want to get in touch with Inez.

chapter four

On Saturday morning, riding the bus to the provincial tryouts, I listened to Bedouin Soundclash on my iPod. It's reggae with enough rock to pump it up. It's the music I use to get into my Zone. Lots of guys listen to rap, but rap is all sharp edges, you know? Reggae is smooth. You want to play basketball, you've gotta be smooth.

The other thing that was getting me into my Zone was thinking about the new basketball shoes in my gym bag. We're talking carbon-fiber arch supports, thermal plastic midsole protection, zoom air cushioning and Michael Jordan's signature on the toes. Sweet. Two hundred and fifty bucks they cost me. I say *me*, because I paid for them myself. A whole week's paycheck from my summer job selling popsicles and candy bars at the corner convenience store. I had to buy them, because my dad and mom said they weren't going to waste two hundred and fifty dollars on a pair of shoes. Waste? Man, parents are so clueless.

It was a good thing I was in my Zone when I got to the locker room at Ottawa U, because once I got into that locker room, I kept bumping into guys' armpits. I don't know where so many six-and-a-half-foot sixteen-year-olds came from. Either these guys were taking growth hormones, or they were fudging their birth certificates. I mean, I'm not a shrimp—and I'm for sure getting a growth spurt next summer—but these guys were so big, they needed binoculars to check if their shoes were tied.

Luckily, I spotted my buddy Mike in a corner of the locker room. Mike plays pickup at the park with me, and he's half an inch shorter than I am. He says we're the same height because half inches don't count, but everyone knows there's a difference between five ten and five ten and a half. That's just mathematics.

Mike and I threw a little banter back and forth while we were getting dressed. That helped calm the tension. It's hard not to look stupid when you walk into a room full of guys and you don't know *anyone*. I mean, some guys can pull off that I'm-so-cool-I-don't-have-to-talk-to-any-of-you-losers attitude, but that's not my style. I laced up my shoes, and then Mike and I eased into the gym for some warm-ups. At nine o'clock sharp, the coach blew his whistle to start the practice.

Coach Donovan was a tall, muscular dude with a skeptical look. He said "Whatcha got?" a lot, like he was waiting for someone to show him something really spectacular.

Spectacular? Wait till he saw my slam dunk. It was going to blow him away.

Coach Donovan explained the procedure: the tryouts for the Ottawa area would take place over three Saturdays. Half an hour after each session, he'd post a list with the names of the guys invited back for the next tryout. The final twelve guys would make up the Ottawa team. They'd travel to Toronto for a four-day development camp and tournament against the other teams from across the province. At the end of the camp, the provincial head coach would pick a team of twelve guys to represent Ontario at the Nationals.

After his speech we went straight into wind sprints. Mike and I grinned at each other as we lined up at the baseline. We had this rivalry about who was faster. Usually Mike beat me by about a stride, but this time I was gunning for him. We ran five wind sprints and he beat me three to two, but we were both way ahead of the pack of six-and-a-half-footers. Those tall guys, they've got long legs but they don't know how to move 'em.

Next we did dribbling and passing drills, then some one-on-one. I kept getting paired up with these guys who were so tall they could have wiped their noses on the top of my head. But I just flowed around them, like water around a rock. Deke left, move right. Ball through the legs. Around the back. Plant and spin. I was in the Zone. I would have given a million bucks to see what Coach Donovan was writing on his clipboard. I had a feeling it was good.

Fifteen minutes before the end, Coach Donovan split us up into teams of five.

"All right, listen up! I want to see full court, five-on-five. Shirts and skins. First team to ten points wins. Winners face the next challengers. Losers hit the showers. Got it? Good. Show me whatcha got."

We took our places for the jump ball. I was feeling all revved up. Mike was on my team—shirts—and that was cool. Mike and I had been playing together so much, we could almost read each other's minds.

We took possession right away, and Mike set up a pick-and-roll. I passed it to him when he came off the pick, and he sank a shot off the backboard. Two points. The skins team evened the score on the next play. Then we went on the offensive again. I passed to the low post, who drove hard to the basket for a layup to make it 4–2. But the skins tied the game again on the next play. It went that way for a while, back and forth. I scored once on a give-and-go with Mike, and our center landed a sweet jump shot. It was tied 8–8 and we were on the defensive when the skins tried for a three-point shot that rebounded off the rim. Our center plucked it out of midair and slung a pass at me that I grabbed on the fly, already making a break down the court.

It was Mike and me on the fast break, two-on-one against a skins' defenseman. I was closing in on the top of the key, with the defenseman stuck to me like glue, when I saw Mike. He was wide open at the bottom of the key and calling for the ball.

One sharp pass to Mike, and we'd clinch the win. But then I heard Coach Donovan's voice in my head: *Whatcha got, kid? Whatcha got?* And I thought: *I'll show you what I've got.*

I blasted through the key toward the basket. Stepped left, picked up the ball, planted my right foot and drove up with my left knee. In the air, I passed the ball under my left knee, around my back, into my right hand, lifted it high toward the basket and...*Wham!* The skins' defenseman slammed his hand on the top of the ball. Stuffed me. It was like I hit a brick wall. I stopped dead in midair. Then I started falling backward. The ball slipped out of my hand. I hit the floor with my butt and looked up to see the skins' defenseman jump over me and swipe the loose ball out of the air. As I sprawled there on my back with my feet waving in the air, even my new shoes looked stupid and useless. I heard the ball hammering against the floor as the skins' player drove down the court. I knew by the cheers a few seconds later that he'd sunk the shot and won the game.

Next thing I knew, Mike was reaching down to help me up.

"I was wide open, man," he said. That made me feel worse than ever. A second ago I just felt stupid for missing my slam dunk. Now I felt like a jerk for not passing to Mike. For not giving him his chance to score.

"Sorry, man," I said. Mike just shook his head and turned to go to the locker room. I was slinking along behind him, not looking at the other guys on our team, when Coach Donovan called me aside.

"Amaro!"

"Sir?" I tried to sneak a glance at his clipboard, but all I could see was the back of it. A million bucks would have been cheap to see what he'd written next to my name. *Idiot? Loser?*

"I'll see you back here next week," he growled. "But let me give you a tip: guys who aren't team players don't make the final cut."

chapter five

Monday after school, Inez and her mom showed up to practice like nothing had happened. When I got to the gym, Inez was sitting on the bench tying her shoelaces. The other girls were stretching or taking shots at the net. Mrs. Ramirez stood in the doorway of the phys-ed teachers' office, watching them.

I took a seat next to Inez. It was noisy in the gym, with all those basketballs hitting the backboard and bouncing off the floor, so I had to sit pretty close to her. Not like I was glued against her or anything, but close enough that I didn't have to yell. Sitting down next to a girl and yelling at her, that's not cool.

"Hey, *cómo estás?*" I said. That's "How's it going?" in Spanish.

Inez finished tying her shoelace and straightened up. Her cheekbone was still purple and green, but at least her eye wasn't swollen shut anymore. She had dark brown eyes with long lashes.

"*Mejor*," she said. Better.

Then she looked away and bent down to tie the other shoelace. I picked up a ball from under the bench and started moving it around in my hands. I was thinking about asking if she was up for a little one-on-one when we were both distracted by the sound of high-heeled shoes crossing the gym floor. You're not supposed to wear high-heeled shoes in the gym. I guess the secretary, Mrs. Dobrinsky, didn't know that. She walked toward Inez's mother, holding out an envelope.

Inez stopped tying her shoelace. She lifted her head and stared across the gym. We were too far away to hear what the secretary said, but we could see Mrs. Ramirez open the envelope and pull out a sheet of paper. She looked at the paper and her face pinched together like she was angry and worried at the same time.

Inez jumped up from the bench and started walking across the gym toward her mom. Mrs. Ramirez saw her coming. She ripped up the paper and threw the pieces into a wastepaper basket beside the office door. Before Inez could reach her, Mrs. Ramirez blew her whistle. "Okay, girls, three laps around the gym. Let's go!"

The girls started jogging around the gym. Inez slowed down. Then she stopped and stood in the middle of the court, staring at her mom. Ifrah jogged up to her and said something. Inez gave her head a shake. Then they both fell in with the other girls and the practice started.

It wasn't the kind of practice you could just blow off. I mean, the girls had their first playoff game coming up on Thursday. Still, I was having trouble concentrating. All I could think about was the look on Mrs. Ramirez's face when she read that letter and the way she ripped it up when she saw Inez coming toward her.

I spent most of the practice thinking about what to do about that letter. When the hour was finally up, I had a plan. While Mrs. Ramirez went into a huddle with the girls to talk strategy, I collected up the loose balls in a big string bag for storage. It was always my job to take the balls back into the equipment room at the end of practice. The only way to get to the equipment room was through the phys-ed teachers' office. That was critical to my plan.

When I passed through the office door, I just reached down and scooped up the wastepaper basket. Then I carried the balls and the basket into the equipment room. Smooth.

The room was dim and jammed with so much gear you could hardly move. I shoved the wastepaper basket behind some gym mats, just in case someone came in. Then I hung the bag of basketballs on its hook. I looked around, but no one had followed me.

I am the straightest guy you'd ever want to meet. I've never even swiped a pack of gum from a corner store. But now? I felt like a teenage criminal. I grabbed the ripped-up scraps of paper out of the wastepaper basket and shoved them into my pocket. Then I grabbed the wastepaper basket, held it behind my back and sauntered into the phys-ed teachers' office.

The girls' huddle was just breaking up. In a second, Mrs. Ramirez would turn around and head back toward the office to pick up her purse. My heart was pounding, like when you're racing down the court on a fast break and there's a big defenseman gaining on you.

I spotted a paper bag with a half-eaten lunch in it sitting on the phys-ed teacher's desk. I grabbed it and emptied it into the wastepaper basket. Even if Mrs. Ramirez decided she wanted that letter back, I doubted she'd dig around under some-one's half-eaten lunch to get it. Then I shoved the wastepaper basket back into its spot beside the door and walked out into the gym, trying to act like everything was cool.

That walk across the gym to the guys' change room was the longest walk of my life. I kept expecting to hear Mrs. Ramirez's voice shout out my name. But she didn't, and finally I pushed open the change-room door and slipped inside.

The place was empty. I sat down on a bench to get my nerves back. My hands were shaking like your ninety-year-old Grandpa's. I heard this *tap-tap-tapping*, and for a second it spooked me. Then I real-ized it was my own foot, tapping against the floor. I got up and splashed cold water on my face. Then I dried my face on a towel that some dude had left hanging on a hook near the showers. The towel didn't smell too good, but that was the least of my problems. I pulled the scraps of paper out of my pocket and laid them on the counter beside the sink.

It wasn't hard to fit the note back together. It was written in black pen, in big capital letters: *DON'T DO ANYTHING STUPID. THIS IS A WARNING.*

chapter six

"*Don't do anything stupid. This is a warning.* What's that supposed to mean?" said Ifrah, when I showed her the note.

"I don't know, Ifrah," I said. "But you don't send someone a warning unless you plan on hurting them."

I'd called Ifrah on her cell phone and asked her to meet me at Cinnamon's, alone. I had to talk to someone about the note. Ifrah was the least likely to freak out. Maddy would be text messaging the whole school within ten seconds. Brenda would want to punch someone's face in.

"So what are you thinking, Slam?" Ifrah said.

"Someone already gave Inez a black eye," I answered. "What if they're planning on doing something worse?"

"But why?" said Ifrah.

"Maybe to keep her out of the playoffs," I said.

Ifrah read the note again and took a slurp of her frappa-thingy. "But the secretary gave the note to Mrs. Ramirez, not to Inez."

"Maybe it was supposed to be for Inez, but the secretary just gave it to her mom," I said. "And her mom opened it, and didn't want Inez to see it. Didn't want to freak her out."

"Maybe," said Ifrah. "But I still don't get it. *Don't do anything stupid.* What does that mean?"

"I've got an idea about that," I said.

"Okay, shoot."

I'd had some time to work out my theory, and now I laid it out for Ifrah.

"Okay, Glebe knows we're the only team that's good enough to beat them in the finals. So obviously, they want us eliminated, right?"

"Makes sense." Ifrah nodded.

"So, let's say number 20 girl gave Inez that black eye in the Sunday pickup game. Then, let's say she told Inez she was gonna do something even worse to her if Brookfield made it to the finals. So Brookfield better not make it to the finals. Get it?"

"So she told Inez to throw the playoffs?" said Ifrah.

"Yeah, to get us eliminated, so Glebe can play some lame team in the final game."

"And she sent Inez this note to remind her?"

"Yeah, threaten her. Like, mess with her mind," I said.

"And if Inez doesn't go along with it?"

"You know how easy it is to break someone's nose in a game? An elbow hard in the face on a rebound, make it look like an accident."

"You think she'd really do that?"

"Everyone knows number 20 plays dirty," I said.

Ifrah frowned.

"It makes sense, Slam. But you haven't got any evidence."

Ifrah and her evidence. It was like we were in court or something.

"What about this?" I tapped my finger on the note. "Can't you get fingerprints off it or something?"

Ifrah looked at the note. It was pretty crumpled-up from being in my pocket. Plus, I'd taped it back together with first-aid tape from the emergency kit in the guys' change room.

"You're supposed to handle evidence carefully, Slam," Ifrah said.

"I'll remember that next time," I said. "But what do we do now?"

"I don't think we can do anything unless we can prove who sent it."

Prove who sent it. I spent the whole walk home from the coffee shop thinking about how to prove that number 20 sent that note to Inez. I tried to picture the envelope, lying in the wastepaper basket before I dumped the half-eaten lunch on top of it. As far as I could remember, there was no stamp on it. That meant that someone had delivered it by hand to the school office. And *that* meant that, even though we didn't have any evidence, we had something else.

We had a witness.

The next morning, I went to talk to the secretary, Mrs. Dobrinsky, in the school office. She had red hair piled up on top of her head and more rings on her fingers than a rapper at the American Music Awards. The stones were probably fake, but they gave me a chance to slip her a compliment. That was Part One of my plan: soften her up.

"Nice bling, Mrs. Dobrinsky," I said.

"Can I help you?" she said. She wasn't exactly warming up to my charm.

"Yeah, hey, I'm Salvador Amaro, the assistant coach of the girls' basketball team." Part Two: establish my cred.

"So the girls have their quarter-final game on Thursday, and I thought it would be cool if you could make an announcement. Tell people to come on out to the game."

"If you'd like to write something down, I could add it to the morning announcements," she said. "Something short."

"Yeah, cool."

I borrowed a pen and paper from her desk and started writing. That was Part Three of my plan: distraction. See, it's like faking a pass. You fake to the right to get the defender off-balance; then you pass to the left where he's not expecting it. I figured Mrs. Dobrinsky wasn't going to tell me who left the note if I just marched up and asked her. But if she thought I was really there about the announcement, then I could slip in a question about the note and catch her off guard. Fake right, pass left. So I asked in a real casual voice, "Oh, Mrs. Dobrinsky, that kid who dropped off the envelope for Mrs. Ramirez yesterday. Did she leave a name?"

"Kid?" Mrs. Dobrinsky looked like she didn't know what I was talking about.

"Yeah, the one that dropped off that envelope yesterday."

"I don't know anything about a kid. A man dropped off an envelope. I delivered it to Mrs. Ramirez. If she was expecting something else...?"

"Yeah, no, I mean, that's cool," I said. I shoved the paper back at her and made for the office door.

"I'll have to correct some of the grammar in this announcement," Mrs. Dobrinsky's voice called after me.

Grammar? Whatever. I had something more important on my mind. I thought I was deking Mrs. Dobrinsky out, and now she'd turned around and deked me out.

A man? What man was she talking about?

49

chapter seven

I kept the information to myself for the next couple of days. I could have told Ifrah, but there was no point in distracting her before the quarter-final game against Hillcrest High. Man, I just wanted to mop the floor with them. Get some confidence going into the semis, you know? I could tell the girls were thinking the same thing. When I got to the gym after school on Thursday, they were pumped.

Inez was planted at the top right corner of the key, shooting baskets. She nailed five in a row. Then she moved to the top left corner and sank three from there. Her eye was almost healed. There was just a little purple shadow on her cheekbone. It made her look kind of tough. The expression on her face said she had something to prove. I had a feeling she was going to go out there and prove it.

Mrs. Ramirez gave me the starting lineup, and I passed it on to the ref. When the game got going, I put a fresh stats sheet on my clipboard and settled in to watch the action.

You can tell right away which teams have talent and which teams have grit. Hillcrest didn't have a lot of talent. But grit? They had it down to the fingernails. Those girls fought for every rebound, every loose ball, every turnaround, every interception.

Their problem was Inez. Inez had talent. And grit. And like I said, Inez was playing like she had something to prove.

If a Hillcrest girl took off on a fast break, Inez would catch up to her and steal the ball back. And if a Hillcrest defender tried to swipe the ball from Inez? She'd juke her with a crossover and drive straight for the basket.

By the time the buzzer sounded for half-time, my girls were twenty points ahead. They'd eaten Hillcrest for supper and they were still hungry for dessert. I grabbed the water bottles and towels and followed them into the change room.

In games like this, the coach always gives the same talk at halftime. If you were writing a manual of pep talks, you could call it the "great-first-half-but-don't-get-too-cocky" talk. You know, the one where you warn your star players about the dangers of overconfidence. Mrs. Ramirez had just started in on this theme when the door to the locker room swung open and Mrs. Dobrinsky walked in carrying a small box wrapped in brown paper.

"I'm sorry to interrupt, Juanita, but the fellow who dropped this off said it was important."

"That's all right, Glenna," Mrs. Ramirez said. She took the box from the secretary and held one corner with her thumb and forefinger, like it was something dirty.

Mrs. Dobrinsky went out, and Mrs. Ramirez got started on her pep talk again. But I had the feeling that no one was listening. Everyone was looking at the box. Then Inez said, "Open it, Mom."

Mrs. Ramirez ignored her and just kept talking about how a few turnovers and some free throws could make a twenty-point lead melt away. So Inez said it again, louder, "Open it, Mom."

Mrs. Ramirez stopped. She looked at Inez and lowered her voice.

"It's okay, Inez," she said.

"It's not okay. Open it," said Inez.

Nobody moved for a couple of seconds. Nobody said anything. Then Inez lunged forward and yanked the package out of her mom's hand and tore off the brown wrapping paper.

"Inez!" Mrs. Ramirez shouted. Inez ripped the lid off the box, screamed and flung the box away from her. It clattered to the ground. The lid went skittering up against the lockers. Something fell out of the box and lay on the floor in the middle of the circle of girls. It was orange and blue and kind of shiny. For a second I didn't know what it was. Then I realized it was a fish—one of those little tropical fish that you see at pet stores. And it was dead.

Inez was screaming hysterically. Mrs. Ramirez tried to put her arm around her, but she shook her off and ran out of the locker room. Ifrah started to go after her, but Mrs. Ramirez stopped her. Her voice sounded hard and tight.

"Ifrah, we need you for the second half. Anisa, you go." She motioned to a second-stringer. The girl nodded and took off after Inez.

"Maddy, you're on," Mrs. Ramirez continued. "Okay, girls, let's get back out there."

She turned to me while the girls herded out of the locker room.

"Salvador, can you clean up this mess, please?"

"Sure thing, Coach," I said.

I waited till the last girl was out the door, then I looked down at the dead fish, the empty box and the ripped wrapping paper. Out in the gym, the whistle sounded to start the game. But in here, there was another game going on. A game I'd somehow gotten mixed up in, along with Inez and Ifrah and Mrs. Ramirez. I didn't know the rules, I didn't know the strategy. I didn't even know who I was up against.

Worse than that, I didn't know if we could win.

chapter eight

After I got my head back together, I went to the equipment room to dig out a pair of soccer-goalie gloves. First off, I didn't feel like touching a dead fish with my bare hands. Second off, I was thinking about what Ifrah said about evidence, and how you weren't supposed to mess it up. This stuff was the only evidence we had if we were going to figure out what was wrong with Inez and her mom.

I found the gloves and picked up a couple of plastic grocery bags kicking around in the phys-ed teachers' office, and I brought them back into the locker room.

First I picked the fish up off the floor and put it in one of the plastic grocery bags, then tied the bag in a knot at the top. I guess the fish was evidence, but I didn't see how you could get anything like fingerprints off it. So I threw the bag with the fish in the garbage. Then I went after the box and the brown wrapping paper.

The box was navy blue cardboard, about half the size of a shoe box, with no store logo on it. The wrapping paper was plain brown, and there wasn't anything written on it at all. I guessed our only chance was to check for fingerprints. Mrs. Dobrinsky had said a "fellow" dropped off the box. Was it the same guy who dropped off the nasty letter? And if so, who was he? And why was he trying to mess around with our coach and our star player? What about Inez's black eye? Was that connected? Or was it just an accident after all? It looked like my theory about number 20 was way off base. So who else had a beef against Inez?

I put the box and the wrapping paper in a plastic bag. Then I wet one of the gym towels and wiped it around on the floor with the toe of my shoe to get rid of any leftover fish slime. Then I went to look for Inez.

Around the side of the school, there's this low brick wall, about waist high, that separates the parking lot from the bike racks. I found Inez sitting with her back against the wall, her elbows on her knees and her face in her hands. Anisa was sitting next to her with a handful of tissues. Inez must have heard me coming, because she looked up. Her eyes were all red and puffy from crying, and that purple shiner on her cheekbone didn't make her look tough anymore. It made her look like a victim.

I know girls don't like guys to see them when they look like that. I mean, it's not exactly pretty. But it didn't make me think worse of Inez—no way. It just made me madder at whoever was messing with her.

"Hey, you played great out there," I said. She hung her head again and started to sob.

"It's just dirty and cheap, whoever's doing this," I said.

Inez didn't answer. She just shook her head. Then she stood up and started to walk away quickly, almost running. Anisa went after her. That made me feel like a real jerk, you know? Like I'd said something wrong and scared her off. Only I couldn't figure out what it was. I watched Anisa catch up to Inez and put an arm around her shoulders. Then I turned around and went back into the gym.

By the time I got there, it was nearly the end of the fourth quarter. Our team was in meltdown. Hillcrest had cut our lead to eight points. Maddy was struggling to control the offense. Brenda was the only one who looked like she had any grit left. If she hadn't been driving to the basket every other play, we could have said good-bye right there to our playoff chances.

I don't want to lay the team's troubles all on Maddy. She was doing her best out there. The problem was no one was in the Zone. I mean, how can you be in the Zone when a package comes with a dead fish in it and your star point guard gets all freaked out about it? It's not possible. If someone was trying to screw up our playoff chances, they were sure doing a good job.

Hillcrest scored on a breakaway and again on a rebound that should have been ours. The only thing that could stop their scoring streak was the final buzzer. Luckily it went off while we were still ahead, 66–62. It was an ugly win, and the girls knew it. They dragged themselves into the locker room like we'd just been eliminated from the playoffs.

And we would be, for sure, if we played like that in the semifinals.

Not only that, but if Inez didn't get back into the game, she wouldn't be winning any scholarships to summer basketball camp.

chapter nine

I caught up with the girls at Cinnamon's after the game. They were scarfing down chocolate brownies and soda pop. After a game like that, frappa-thingies and biscotti just don't cut it.

Brenda was sitting between Ifrah and Maddy, scraping the chocolate icing off her brownie and eating it with a fork. She held up the fork as I came toward them.

"Don't tell us, Slam. We sucked," she said.

I grabbed a chair and straddled it backward. I'd already decided I wasn't going to rag on the girls. I figured what they needed was some positive energy.

"Hey, you won the game. Now you've gotta move on. Get psyched up for the semis," I said.

"Yeah, if our point guard decides to play," a girl called Sarah grumbled. She was our shooting guard, though she hadn't done much shooting this game.

"It's not Inez's fault," Brenda snapped.

"Yeah, well whose fault is it then?" Sarah said.

I didn't like where this was going. I mean, I've seen it before. A team starts underperforming, and the players start sniping at each other, trying to pin the blame. Then they get out on the court and they can't play together. Because on the court, you've gotta trust your teammate to be there when you snap him a blind pass at a critical moment. How can you do that on the court if you're tearing each other apart in the locker room? It's not possible.

I stepped in before things went any further.

"Have any of you guys talked to Inez?" I said.

The girls shook their heads.

"She wouldn't talk to me. She just took off," said Anisa.

"We should call her at home," said Brenda.

Brenda took out her cell phone and called the number. She listened for maybe thirty seconds. Then she flipped her phone shut.

"That's weird," she said.

"What?" said Ifrah.

"There's no answer."

"That's really weird," said Maddy through a mouthful of chocolate.

"Does anyone know where she lives?" I said.

The girls gave a kind of group shrug.

"She never invited anyone over to her place," Ifrah said.

"Yeah," said Maddy. "She said her dad didn't want her to bring friends home."

I didn't like that. Not that I was going to go stalking Inez, but I figured one of the girls should drop over to see if she was okay. I went to the counter and borrowed a phone book from the barista. I brought it back to the table and flipped to the Rs. There were a couple of dozen listings for *Ramirez*.

"What's the phone number?" I asked Brenda. She punched it up on her cell. It didn't match any of the listings in the book.

"Maybe the number isn't listed," said Ifrah.

"Okay, guys, this is getting really weird," said Maddy.

"But in a way, it makes sense," said Ifrah.

"It doesn't make sense to me!" Maddy said.

"Think about it," Ifrah said. "If someone wanted to mess with Inez's head, why send those notes and packages and stuff to her at school? Why not at home? But obviously, if Inez's address isn't listed in the phone book..."

"I knew I should have punched her in the face," Brenda cut in.

"Who?" said Maddy. "What are you guys talking about?"

"That number 20 Glebe girl," said Brenda. "I should have taken her out, right after she gave Inez that black eye."

"You don't even know if it was her," Ifrah pointed out. "Besides, didn't you hear what Mrs. Dobrinsky said? She said it was a man who dropped off the package today."

"Okay." Brenda jutted out her chin. "Well, if it wasn't number 20, maybe it was the Glebe coach."

I'd actually thought about that, but I didn't buy it.

"Coaches don't go around sending people dead fish just so they can win the playoffs," I said.

"Maybe he's a psycho," said Maddy.

"He's been coaching there for a long time," I said. "If he was psycho, I think someone would have figured it out by now."

"Okay, Slam," Brenda pointed her fork at me. "Have you got another idea?"

"I've got something better than an idea. I've got evidence."

I pulled the plastic shopping bag out of my gym bag and opened it so the girls could see the box and the brown wrapping paper inside.

"Oh, Slam, that's sick! There was a dead fish in there," said Maddy. She turned away like she was going to gag.

"Can you get prints off it, Ifrah?" I said.

"I can try. I've got a kit at home," said Ifrah.

"Great, so what do we do next?" said Brenda. "Fingerprint every guy in Ottawa till we see whose prints match?"

"Hey, at least I got the evidence," I said. I didn't need Brenda giving me attitude.

Brenda pressed her finger into a blob of chocolate icing on her plate. Then she made a chocolate fingerprint on the table.

"Doesn't matter, Slam," she said. "Doesn't do us any good without a suspect."

chapter ten

There's this T-shirt I saw in a sports store once. It's got the word *TEAM* written in big letters, and underneath, in smaller letters, is the word *me.* Get it? The *TEAM* is bigger than *me.* I was thinking about that motto as I rode the bus to the second session of the provincial tryouts Saturday morning. This time I was going to show Coach Donovan that I knew how to be a team player.

One good thing about Mike is he doesn't hold a grudge. When I came up to him in the locker room, he gave me a high five and a "hey, how's it going." There were not as many guys in the locker room this time, only about thirty. But there was more tension. Guys were checking out other guys from the corners of their eyes. Measuring them up to figure out who was going to get cut and who was going to be left standing.

At 9:00 AM sharp, Coach Donovan blew his whistle. He put us through ten minutes of warm-ups and stretching, and then he blew the whistle again.

"All right, boys. Anyone who wants to play on the provincial team has to be in top physical condition. So here's your chance to show me whatcha got. We'll start with wind sprints. Three sets of ten. On the baseline. Go!"

After wind sprints, we did five minutes of jumping jacks. Fifty push-ups. A hundred sit-ups. Ten minutes of skipping rope. It was like he was trying to eliminate guys by making them drop dead.

When Coach Donovan blew his whistle again, the sweat was pouring down my face, like lava running down a volcano. This time, he called us around a chalkboard and started showing us offensive plays.

There's something about chalkboards. Start drawing Xs and Os on a chalkboard, and you might as well be drawing a molecular diagram for chemistry class. What I mean is they make my brain kind of tune out. Coach Donovan had the board divided into three sections with three separate offensive plays. I was really trying to keep track of them. But two minutes after he finished explaining them, I couldn't remember which one had the winger coming across the key to set a screen for the shooting guard and which one started with a pass to the power forward on a sharp cut.

Coach Donovan divided us into shirts and skins again, five-on-five. Mike was on my team, along with three guys I didn't know.

"Okay, boys. This is how it's going to work. When the point guard crosses the centerline, I call out 'one,' 'two' or 'three.' I want you guys to run the play that I call. Got it? Good. Show me whatcha got!"

It was going to take some quick thinking for me to save my bacon on this one. The skins won the jump, so we went on defensive for the first play. They scored. I caught the ball on a throw-in from our center and started bringing it up the court.

When I passed the centerline, Coach Donovan called out, "Two! Number two!"

I tried to picture the chalkboard with play number two, but it was just a mess of circles and arrows in my head. So I forgot about the chalkboard and looked to the frontcourt instead to see what Mike and the guys were doing.

I figured I'd just keep the ball alive until someone got free and called for it. If I could get the pass to him, I'd done my job.

If I could get the pass to him. That was the problem. See, basketball's all about timing. Sometimes there's only a split second when a guy manages to shake free from his defender, and the ball has to be in his hands, *bang!* Like that. What I mean is it's all about anticipation. And since I couldn't remember the plays, my anticipation was gone. Didn't exist, man. Nowhere to be found.

Three times I brought the ball up the court and twice my passes got intercepted. I knew I was headed for Nowhereville unless I did something to turn it around.

So the next time, I didn't listen when I crossed the centerline and Coach Donovan called out, "Three! Number three!" I had my own plan.

Ten feet from the top of the key, I pulled a behind-the-back crossover, put on the jets and blew past my defender to the inside. Mike was on the left wing, so I knew his defender would pinch in to cover me as I drove for the basket. And that's exactly what happened. Two steps into the paint, I went up like I was going for the jump shot. But instead of shooting, I dished the ball back to Mike on the outside. He was totally in the clear. Mike took the set shot and *swoosh!* Two points. Just like that, I was back in the Zone.

It felt so good I didn't even hear Coach Donovan call the play when I brought the ball up the court the next time. I already knew what I was going to do. I made this signal to Mike that we used in street ball, and he nodded. It was going to be sweet.

This time when I got to the top of the key, I cut to the right to draw the defenders. Mike ran down the left side of the key to take up a position at the low post. I faked a pass to the guy on the right wing. Then I turned and lobbed the ball high over the key toward Mike. Mike jumped, caught the ball in midair and didn't even come down with it. He just alley-ooped it into the basket. Sweet.

The ball had hardly hit the floor when a whistle blasted. Coach Donovan shouted, "Amaro!"

"Yo, Coach, sir!" I shouted back. I was still way deep in the Zone.

"Was that the play I called, Amaro?"

"No, sir. That was straight out of the playbook of my mind!"

"You want to explain that, Amaro?"

"It's called feeling, Coach. See, I'm not

really a playbook kind of guy. I'm a feeling kind of guy."

"Yeah? Well, see how you like the feeling of your backside on the bench," Coach Donovan looked at his clipboard and called out the name of another point guard. "Yousof, you're on."

A guy came jogging onto the court. It took me a second to realize what was happening. Benched! I pull the sweetest move those tryouts had seen, and the coach benches me. Man, it wasn't fair.

I wasn't even hogging the glory. Didn't I let Mike take the shot? Twice in a row? I was being a team player. And this was what I got for it. Benched. All I could say was that Coach Donovan was an idiot.

The list of guys who'd made the cut was supposed to be up half an hour after the end of the session, but forty-five minutes after we'd hit the showers, we were still waiting. It was almost an hour before Coach Donovan came into the hallway and taped it up to the wall. I had to elbow my way through the tall guys to get to the front of the crowd and see what it said.

The first thing I noticed was the numbers one to twenty along the left-hand side of the page. I scanned down the names on the list. Mike was there at number eight. I had to look a lot farther to find my name.

It was number twenty. The last name on the list.

chapter eleven

Mrs. Ramirez didn't show up to teach Spanish class on Monday. Inez wasn't at school either, and when I tried calling the home number that Brenda had given me, it just rang and rang. No answer and no voice mail. By the time the team hit the gym for practice at 3:45, I was starting to wonder how we were going to handle our semifinal game on Thursday if Inez and her mom were still AWOL.

I heard somewhere that when you're a coach, the first thing you've got to do is identify your team's strengths. Like, if you've got a super-quick guy on your team, then you try to create opportunities for the fast break. But if you've got a bunch of players that are tall and slow, you don't try for the breakaways. You just crush the other team with your height advantage. I had never really thought too deeply about that kind of stuff when I was just Slam the Player. But now that I was Slam the Coach, I had to develop an offensive strategy. And I had to do it quickly, because the game was in three days.

I got the girls set up with a three-on-three drill. Then I grabbed a clipboard and a pen from the phys-ed teachers' office to make some notes. I'd just started to work out an offense when Ifrah came up to me.

"Hey, Slam, look up there." She jerked her head up at the stands.

The stands in the Brookfield gym look down on the court, and you get to them by a back stairway that leads off the hall. Unless it's a game night, they're usually empty. That's why it was so strange to see a man up there.

He wasn't a teacher or a coach, at least not one that I knew. For a second, I thought he might be a scout, but scouts are slick-looking. This guy was big and heavy and rough-looking. He had thick black hair and a meaty face. His shirt was half tucked into his pants. He was leaning against the front-row railing on thick hairy arms, drinking beer from a can and glaring down at the girls.

He had a mean look in his eye. The kind of look that makes you want to duck, because any second he might take a swing at you. He dropped his beer can onto the floor. Then he turned around, kind of unsteady on his feet, and climbed the steps to the exit. I looked at Ifrah.

"I'm going after him," I said. "Can you run the practice?"

"No problem," she nodded.

I grabbed my backpack from under the bench and slid out the gym door.

When I caught up to the guy, he was crossing the road toward the bus shelter. There were a couple of other people waiting for the bus, so I slipped into the crowd.

My plan was to follow the guy home and see what I could find out about him. I didn't know for sure that he was the guy harassing Inez and her mom, but like Brenda said, we needed a suspect. He was the most suspicious thing I'd seen.

The guy got off at a stop in front of a run-down strip mall. There was a dentist's office, a junky-looking convenience store and one of those places that gives out instant loans. The guy walked around to the back of the mall, kind of swaying on his feet. Then he climbed a dirt footpath up a little hill.

He was headed toward a big apartment building, one of those brown-brick high-rises with rows of boxy concrete balconies crammed with bikes and barbecues. I followed him at a distance, trying not to look too obvious.

Next to the entrance of the apartment building was a sign that said *Billingsview Terrace*. The letters on the sign were all swoopy, but the paint was peeling off. On either side of the entrance doors there was a patch of grass overgrown with dandelions and a concrete planter with cigarette butts sticking up out of the dirt instead of flowers.

Like most apartment buildings, this one had two doors. The first door was unlocked and led into a little foyer with a panel showing the names of all the building's tenants, a buzzer beside each name. A second, locked door, led into the main lobby.

I watched the guy go inside the first door, take out a set of keys and let himself through the second door. The door locked behind him. I thought about checking out the panel of tenants' names, but how would I know which one was his? Besides, there were a couple of guys hanging around outside the entrance, smoking and giving me that what're-you-doing-here-kid look. So I turned around and headed back to the bus stop.

Later that evening, Ifrah called.

"Hey, Slam. You follow that guy home?" she said.

"Yeah, he lives in this big apartment building. Billingsview Terrace."

"Never heard of it," said Ifrah. "But guess what? I picked up the beer can he left in the stands. His fingerprints were all over it."

"Yeah?"

"Yeah. And they matched the prints on that box with the dead fish."

"Looks like he's our guy."

"Yeah," she said, "but who is he?"

Ifrah and I tossed around some theories. We hung up after we got tired of going in circles.

The way I saw it, the only person who might be able to tell us what was going on was Inez. But where was Inez? I didn't want to sound like somebody's dad, but I was starting to get worried about her.

So I went on Trixie Hoopster's Facebook page and sent her a message.

Where r u? r u ok?

chapter twelve

There's a buzz that fills the gym in the last few minutes before an important game. The *thwack* of basketballs in warm-up. The scoreboard lighting up. The smell of sweat and the squeak of rubber-soled shoes on the court. It keys you up. Makes you feel spring-loaded. I was pacing back and forth behind the bench, hoping my offensive strategy wasn't going to crash and burn. Wishing the game would hurry up and start, and at the same time wishing we had way more time to prepare for it.

It was the semifinal game against Lisgar, and Inez and her mom hadn't shown up. In fact, no one had seen them or heard from them all week. I had this sick, nervous feeling in my stomach. I tried to tell myself I wasn't nervous about Inez; I was just nervous about the game.

I'd spent the past two days figuring out my offensive strategy and practicing it with the girls. Now the only thing I could do was focus on the game.

Then the ref blew his whistle, and a minute later Ifrah was taking the jump ball.

It was obvious from the first few minutes that the teams were about equally matched for skills. But Lisgar was playing cool, like they had their heads together. Our girls were jumpy, making up plays on the fly. If we could settle down and start running our offense, I was pretty confident we had a shot at winning. Don't panic, you know? Run the play and keep running it, and pretty soon the points would start racking up.

But halfway into the first quarter, our offense wasn't coming together. It was like the girls had totally forgotten it.

See, the offense I'd come up with gave the girls three opportunities to score. It started with Brenda coming down to set a screen for Ifrah at the low post. Then Ifrah would pop out into the center of the key for a pass and a quick shot. That was scoring opportunity number one.

If Maddy couldn't get the ball to Ifrah, then the girl on the right wing was supposed to cut to the outside for a pass and a jump shot. Opportunity number two.

If she didn't get free for a pass, at least the cut would draw her defender to the outside. That made room at the top of the key for Brenda to pop back up and receive a pass, then turn and shoot or drive for the basket. Opportunity number three.

In practice, it came together perfectly. But it all started with Brenda coming down to set the screen for Ifrah. Now Brenda wasn't setting the screen. Instead she was calling for the ball on the wing and taking jump shots. Some of the shots went in, but the problem was it left everyone else standing around doing nothing. And you can't win a game if most of your players are doing nothing.

The score was 10–8 for Lisgar when I called a time-out.

"Good work out there, girls," I said. "Now, let's focus on running our offense. Brenda, remember, it starts with you coming down to set a screen for Ifrah."

"I know how the offense goes, Slam," Brenda interrupted. I didn't like the snarl in her voice. Like I'd dissed her or something.

"Okay, then how come you're not running it?"

"Don't rag on me, Slam, I'm the only one scoring points out there."

"Maybe that's because you're not giving anyone else a chance," I said.

"Oh yeah? Who died and made you king?"

Man, what was her problem? Whatever it was, I didn't have time to fix it in a sixty second time-out. I turned to Anisa, who was sitting on the bench.

"Anisa, can you run the play?"

"Sure thing, Coach," she said.

The ref's whistle sounded.

"Okay, Anisa, get out there," I said. "Brenda, you're on the bench."

I could feel Brenda's bad vibes drilling into me, like voodoo or something. But the coach has to see the big picture, you know? Players, sometimes they just see their own glory. That's what gives them attitude. And yeah, sometimes attitude is what lets you make spectacular plays. But in the end too much of it can ruin a team. And if you asked me, Brenda had way too much attitude.

By the beginning of the second quarter, our offense was working great as long as Ifrah or Sarah got the pass. The problem was with Anisa. She could set the screen all right. But if Maddy passed her the ball, that ball was as good as dead. Anisa's jump shot looked like something out of kindergarten. She didn't have the aggression to drive to the basket for a layup. Plus, she was weak on defense. Brenda was our best defensive player. And there she was, getting splinters in her backside instead of burning rubber on the court.

By halftime, Lisgar was ahead, 32–26. I needed Brenda back in the game. But Brenda wasn't talking to me. So I sent Ifrah to have a word with her while I gave the rest of the girls some water and a pep talk.

"She doesn't like the way you just walked in and took over the team," Ifrah reported back to me after her little one-on-one with Brenda.

"What do you mean *took over the team?*" I said. I couldn't follow that logic with a GPS.

"You know, after Inez and her mom took off. How you just came in and told everyone what the offense was going to be and how we were going to run it."

"But Ifrah, I'm the coach."

"Assistant coach," she said.

"Assistant to who, Ifrah?" I said. "'Cause I'm looking around here and I don't see any other coaches in the room."

Sure, we'd convinced the music teacher, Mr. Davies, to fill in as our teacher-supervisor, but he didn't know anything about basketball. Right now he was sitting on the bench with his eyes closed, chilling to the tunes on my iPod.

Ifrah sighed like I was being thick-headed.

"Come on, Slam. She just wanted you to consult with the rest of us, you know?"

Consult? Was this basketball or group therapy?

"Well, can you go consult her to get her butt back on the court and run the offense?" I said. "'Cause if she doesn't, we're going to get consulted right out of the finals."

"I'll see what I can do," said Ifrah.

Finally the girls convinced Brenda to get back in the game and run the offense. She still wouldn't talk to me, but I didn't care. I had my A-team back on the court. And a shot at winning the game.

chapter thirteen

The girls played hard the whole second half. They ran our offense, and a full-court, man-to-man D. But every time we evened the score, Lisgar would pull ahead again. With three minutes left in the game, we were trailing 50–54.

Maddy had the ball in the frontcourt. She was trying to keep it alive while the other girls set up our offense, but the Lisgar defender was bugging her like a kid sister on a long car trip. Maddy was getting tired.

Brenda ran down to set the screen for Ifrah. Ifrah made her move into the key, but Ifrah's defender slipped past the screen and blocked the passing lane. Trouble was Maddy had already picked up the ball to pass. Now, she needed to get rid of it. She twisted back and forth on her pivot foot, looking for an open player. Finally, she threw a desperate pass to the right wing. The Lisgar defender grabbed it out of midair and took off on a breakaway.

Maddy turned and started to run after her. The Lisgar girl crossed the centerline, driving hard. By the time she reached the three-point line, Maddy was so far behind I was ready to call for Search and Rescue. But that was no excuse for what Maddy did next. She stopped running and started to walk, while the Lisgar girl went straight for a layup and two points.

That is not what you're supposed to do in that situation. I mean, what if the Lisgar girl had missed? What if there was a rebound and a chance to turn it around? Maddy should have been chasing that girl like a cop chasing a graffiti punk. I don't care *how* far behind she was. But I knew what Maddy was thinking. She was thinking: *Why should I chase her? We're not going to win anyway.*

See, she was thinking like we'd already lost the game. Thinking that we tried our best. We made it to the semifinals. It wasn't our fault if our point guard went missing in the middle of the playoffs. It wasn't our fault if our coach walked out on us. No one could blame us for losing the game.

Those aren't the kinds of thoughts anyone's supposed to be thinking when you've still got a chance to win. But I knew Maddy was thinking them because I caught myself thinking the same things. Thinking that no one could blame *me* if the girls lost. I didn't *have* to step in as coach. I could have just blown the whole team off after Mrs. Ramirez left. At least we tried.

See, my mind was already making up all kinds of excuses to make me feel better for losing. Then I looked up in to the stands, and I caught sight of the guy from Billingsview Terrace. The guy who was messing with Inez.

He was standing near the exit door, leaning with one hand against the wall and turning his head back and forth. Looking all around the gym. Looking for something. Or someone.

I thought about the mean look in his eyes and the dead fish he'd sent to Mrs. Ramirez, and it made me mad. Fired me up, you know? So as soon as we took possession, I motioned to Maddy to call a time-out.

The girls were panting and sweating when they came to the bench. They grabbed the water bottles and squirted water all over their heads and into their mouths.

"Listen girls," I said. "There's two minutes left. You've got to dig deeper. You've got to really want this."

"We're trying, Slam," said Maddy. "But what's the point? We're not going to win the finals without Inez."

"That's thinking like a loser, Maddy. You've got to think like a winner," I said. "Listen. Someone out there is messing with Inez. And if he's messing with her, he's messing with all of us. 'Cause we're a team, right? So are we going to let him win, or are we going to fight back?"

"Fight!" Ifrah shouted. It was good to have her on my side, especially after my scrap with Brenda.

"Everyone!" I shouted back.

"Fight!" Brenda joined in.

"Louder!"

"Fight!" the girls yelled.

Then the ref blew his whistle, and I sent the girls back onto the court.

Maddy took the ball to the top of the key. The girls set up the offense. Their movements were sharp and aggressive, as if they'd shaken off all the tiredness and found new energy for the last 120 seconds. Ifrah busted free of her defender and called for the pass. Pivot. Jump shot. Off the rim. Ifrah went up for the rebound but a Lisgar girl grabbed it instead. She whipped an overhead pass out of the key to the Lisgar guard. The guard took off, trying for a break, but this time the girls fought back.

Maddy caught her just before the centerline and swiped the ball away on the dribble. The ball bounced toward the sideline, but Maddy scrambled after it and caught it in time. Brenda called for it near the top of the key, and Maddy drilled her an overhead pass. Brenda turned for a quick jump shot. The ball hit the backboard, bounced off the rim. The Lisgar forward went up for the rebound, but this time Ifrah beat her to it. Ifrah snatched the ball from the air, then powered up for the put-back. Off the glass and into the net. 52–56. A Lisgar guard took the throw-in. Our girls stuck tight, trying to deny the inbounding pass. At last the Lisgar guard got a pass away to Brenda's man. The girl had hardly caught the ball when Brenda grabbed it with both hands and ripped it out of her fingers. The Lisgar player looked shocked, like she expected the ref to call a foul. But there was no foul, just a move that Brenda must have learned on the rugby field. Brenda drove to the basket for a layup. 54–56.

Lisgar used a stack-up play to inbound the ball this time, and their point guard took it slowly up the court. There was a minute left to play. I could see they were trying to run down the clock, but it was a risky strategy because the shot clock was running down too. They had to get a shot away, and the more the time ticked down, the more chance they would panic and take one from a bad angle. They passed it around the top of the key for a while but couldn't get it to the inside. Finally one of the guards took a long-range jump shot. It rebounded off the rim—right into Ifrah's hands.

Ifrah drilled the overhead pass to Brenda on the outside. Brenda took off on the break. A Lisgar girl pounded at her heels, but Brenda didn't fumble. She drove over the centerline, past the top of the key. The Lisgar girl cut in front of her to block the shot. But Brenda rammed right into her and kept going for the basket. Layup. Two points, with the Lisgar girl lying on her back on the floor and the ref's whistle shrieking a foul call.

Three seconds left on the clock. I jumped off the bench. If the ref called Brenda for charging, I was going to ream him out. I didn't care if word got back to the provincial team coaches.

"Foul!" the ref called. "Number 24, Lisgar! Foul on the shot!"

Now the Lisgar coach jumped from the bench. She was shouting at the ref, waving her arms. But the ref wasn't going to change his mind. Three seconds left. The game was tied. And now, Brenda went to the free-throw line.

This time it was Lisgar that called the time-out.

The Lisgar girls huddled around their coach. They tried to make like they were plotting some great strategy for the last three seconds of the game, but I didn't buy it. What they were really trying to do was psych Brenda out before she took the free throw.

I didn't call the girls back to our bench. Brenda knew what she had to do, and I figured nothing I said would change that. Besides, last time I checked, Brenda wasn't speaking to me. But then Brenda broke away from the other girls and came over to talk.

"That guy up there in the stands," she jerked her head toward the heavyset man leaning against the wall by the exit door. "Is he the guy messing with Inez?"

I hadn't pointed him out to the girls because I didn't want to distract them from the game, you know? But Brenda must have noticed him anyway. She'd seen him at practice on Monday and put two and two together.

"Yeah," I said. "That's him."

"We're going to beat him, Slam," Brenda said. Her jaw was so tight, I could almost hear her teeth grinding. The ref's whistle blew, and Brenda turned and walked back to the free-throw line.

The ref handed her the ball. She dribbled it once. Her knees were bent low when she picked it up. She fixed her eyes on the basket. In one motion she uncoiled her legs, lifted the ball and sent it soaring toward the basket.

I think my heart stopped beating between the time she released it and the time it swooshed through the net. The next three seconds were a jumble of noise and motion: the squeak of basketball shoes on the court, the girls shouting, gray and blue uniforms blurring back and forth, the ball hitting the hardwood, the sound of the final buzzer. And the final score in lights on the scoreboard: Brookfield 57; Lisgar 56.

The girls screamed. Somebody hugged me. By the time I'd got my head clear, a woman was standing next to me, introducing herself as a scout from Carleton University.

"You've got a lot of talent on this team," she said.

I said, "Yeah." I didn't tell her there was a fair amount of attitude as well.

"I've heard about your point guard, Inez Ramirez. She wasn't out there today?"

"Yeah, Inez got sick." I lied through my teeth. "She's got the flu. But she's going to be here for the finals next week. You should come back."

"Thanks, I will," said the scout. Then she went to talk to Ifrah.

I looked back up into the stands to see if the Billingsview Terrace guy was there. He was the only clue I had that might lead me to Inez. But the exit door was crammed with boyfriends and friends and parents coming down to congratulate the girls on their win. When the crowd cleared, the suspect was gone.

chapter fourteen

On the bus on my way to the provincial tryouts that Saturday, I was thinking about Brenda. See, Ifrah told me after the game that Brenda was surprised I'd benched her. Surprised? Man, she should have been surprised I let her play in the second half. If it hadn't been a must-win game for us, I would have kept her tush on the wood until the final buzzer sounded. Why? Because if you're a player, you don't just go around deciding that you're not going to do what the coach tells you to do. And that made me think about how Coach Donovan benched me after I made that alley-oop pass to Mike last Saturday. At the time, I thought Coach Donovan was an idiot. But now—well, it was pretty tough to admit—but now, I thought that maybe I was the idiot.

Here's the thing: You never know how big your ego is until someone tells you to park it. Then all of a sudden you realize it won't fit into the parking space 'cause you've got an ego as big as a Hummer, and all along you thought it was about the size of a Volkswagen Rabbit. You get what I'm saying? I was feeling pretty humble by the time I poked my head into the locker room at Ottawa U.

It was down to twenty guys now, and everyone knew that by the end of the day, it would be down to twelve. A dozen guys who would get to go to the development camp in Toronto for a shot at making the provincial team.

The guys who knew each other were exchanging high fives and throwing some banter around, but beneath it, everyone was checking each other out. Trying to figure out who would make the final twelve. I caught a couple of guys looking at me like they were already crossing me off their mental lists. As if Coach Donovan putting my backside on the bench last Saturday meant that this Saturday he was going to kick it out the door. Not if I could help it.

The practice started with a drill for shooting three-pointers. You take twenty-five shots, moving in an arc around the three-point line. The guy who sinks the most shots doesn't have to do push-ups at the end of the drill. Everyone else is down for ten.

I could feel I was in the Zone as soon as my shoes left the court for that first jump shot. Swish. Nothing but net. Swish again. Two for two. Soon it was eighteen for twenty. Nineteen. Twenty for twenty-five. That was a good score, nothing to be ashamed of. But another guy racked up twenty-one, so I was down on the floor for push-ups with the rest of the pack.

Some guys did these little wimpy half-push-ups, the kind where you just dip your elbows and bob your head up and down. But I went all the way, arms pumping, nose to the ground. No way Coach Donovan was going to look at me and see a slacker.

Next we did an alternates drill, alternating jump shots from elbow to elbow. After that, we did some one-on-one and three-on-three. By the end of the first hour, I was sweating so much I needed to wring out my socks. But it felt good. Really good.

Coach Donovan blew his whistle and called us over to the chalkboard.

"All right, boys, we're going to go over the plays we learned last week one more time."

He started drawing his Xs and Os on the chalkboard, and for a second I thought, *Man, I am doomed*. But it was only for a second. Because this time I was determined. This time, instead of just seeing Xs and Os, I really tried to visualize the plays. Instead of looking at an X with an arrow pointing across a rectangle on a chalkboard,

I visualized the forward, cutting across the key. It was like I could see it all in 3-D, and suddenly it all made sense. Not only that, but I was committed to the plays. No taking off and doing my own thing this time. This time I was going to do *exactly* what the coach told me.

Coach Donovan split us up into four teams of five.

"Shirts and skins. Point guard calls the play. The game's to twenty. Winners take on the next team, losers hit the showers. Show me whatcha got."

I was the shirts' point guard. As I took up my position, I wondered if Coach Donovan did it on purpose. I mean, put me on the court for the first shift so he could eliminate me quicker. Watch me screw up his plays and scratch me off his list for the camp in Toronto. If that was the case, I was out to prove him wrong.

I caught the ball off the tip from our center and brought it up the court.

"One! Number one!" I called. I pulled a couple of dribbling moves while the guys got set up. Then I watched the winger come across the key and set a screen for the shooting guard. I saw the guard pop out from behind the screen and whipped a pass right into his hands. Jump shot. Two points. I was in the Zone.

It was like those plays were burned into my mind. I could've almost run them with my eyes closed. Number one. Number two. Back to number one. Now number three. And if the play fell apart, take a quick jump shot from the top of the key, or deke out the defender and drive for the basket. By the end, our team was the last one standing. And when I hit our center with the back-door pass for a bank shot and the final two points, it felt as sweet as sinking the winning basket myself.

"All right everyone, hit the showers!" Coach Donovan shouted.

Forget hitting the showers, I felt like shouting back, *let's hit the road to Toronto.* But I didn't want the coach to think I was getting too cocky, so I just slid in among the group of guys and headed toward the locker room.

"Amaro!" Coach Donovan barked.

"Sir?"

"C'mere."

Every guy in the gym looked at me. It felt awkward walking over to him in front of everyone, like getting sent to the principal's office.

"Yes, sir?" I said. But Coach Donovan didn't say anything else until all the other guys had gone into the locker room. Then he looked up from his clipboard.

"You know I'm taking twelve players to Toronto next week?"

"Yes, sir."

"There's one player I want on my team," he said. "It's the Amaro I saw today. Hard worker. Listens up. Plays smart. But there's another player I don't want. That's the Amaro I saw last week. Talented kid, but a real jerk. Now I want you to tell me, if I put you on the team, which Amaro's going to be getting on the bus to Toronto with me next weekend? The hard worker or the talented jerk?"

He looked at me with that "whatcha got?" look, but this time it wasn't just about basketball moves. I had the feeling if I let him down, I'd be shamed for life. So I tried to look him in the eye as I said, "I'll work really hard, sir. I really want to make the provincial team. It's my dream."

"Every kid here's got that dream, Amaro," he growled. He looked back down at his clipboard. "Okay, hit the showers."

That was the longest shower of my life. I spent more time shampooing my hair than a girl before her first date. It took me that long to work up the nerve to go out and look at the list of guys who made the cut. By the time I got out of the shower and got dressed, there was nobody else in the change room. I stowed my basketball clothes and my new shoes in my gym bag—the shoes that cost me a whole week's paycheck. You make that kind of a sacrifice for a pair of shoes and they should bring you good luck, right? Then I slung the bag over my back and headed out the locker room door.

The list was in its usual spot, taped to the brick wall with a piece of masking tape. The numbers on the left-hand side went from one to twelve.

And there, at number seven, was *Salvador Amaro*.

chapter fifteen

If there was one thing I should have been doing the next morning, it was shooting hoops. I needed all the practice I could get before the development camp in Toronto. But instead, I was on the number 1 bus, riding downtown. Inez had sent me a message on Facebook. *Can u meet me? Rideau ctr food ct, 9am sun.* It was the only thing that could have dragged me away from the basketball court that morning.

I got off the bus at the Rideau Centre, made my way past some grungy-looking people hanging out on the sidewalk and went through the glass doors into the mall. The stores were just opening up, and the food court was almost empty. Inez was sitting way at the back. I picked up a couple of chocolate-glazed donuts from the Tim Hortons counter and made my way toward her through the maze of plastic tables. She didn't look up until I was standing right beside her.

"Hey, *cómo estás?*"

She shrugged, but didn't say anything. I put one of the chocolate-glazed donuts on the table in front of her, next to her cup of coffee.

"I got you a donut. Chocolate, the ultimate breakfast food."

I was trying to make her smile, and I succeeded maybe twenty percent.

"Thanks, Slam," she said.

She was wearing a white T-shirt and a jean jacket and some little gold earrings that looked really pretty against her skin. The bruise on her cheek had faded to almost nothing, but her eyes looked red and tired and kind of sad. She'd put on black eyeliner, which didn't help. Actually, it made her look worse. But I didn't say anything, because I know you don't say that kind of thing to girls.

I sat down on the plastic chair opposite her.

"So we won the semis," I said.

"Yeah, I saw it on the school website."

"You coming out next week to play in the finals?"

"I want to," she said, "but my mom won't let me."

"What's up with that? Your mom's supposed to be the coach."

"Yeah, well." Inez stared into her coffee cup. "My mom and dad are splitting up."

She looked at me like that was supposed to explain everything. But it didn't explain anything at all. I mean, I know lots of guys whose parents split up, and they don't disappear from the face of the earth halfway through the playoffs.

"So," Inez kept on, "my mom and me are staying at this place near here. There's all these counselors and stuff, and I'm supposed to talk to them about my family. I really hate it."

"So why don't you hang with your dad for a while instead?"

Her hand came up to touch the bruise on her cheek.

"My dad's the problem, Slam."

How could I have been so stupid? Now it all made sense: what the girls said about Inez's dad being super strict, how she was afraid to go home after she missed her curfew, how she showed up on Monday with that black eye.

Still, I didn't want to believe it. I mean, her own *dad*.

"I thought you said it was an accident. In a basketball game," I said.

"What was I supposed to tell people, Slam?"

"Did you call the cops?"

"Mom called them after we got out of there. They arrested him—and let him out the next day on bail."

"On bail? That's not right!" I said.

Inez wiped her eyes with the back of her hand. Her black eyeliner smudged across her cheek.

"That's the way it is," she said.

I didn't know what to say. I mean, did her dad hit her just because she missed curfew? Or maybe he told her she was grounded and she talked back. Or maybe her parents were already fighting when she got home, and Inez just got in the way.

In any case, I wasn't going to ask her to explain. Not right there, anyway, in the middle of the Rideau Centre. I mean, how do you tell someone about that kind of stuff? If it was my family, I wouldn't tell anyone about it. Not in a million years.

But I had to say something, so I asked her, "So where are you guys staying? In a hotel or something?"

"I wish," Inez said. "Mom says we can't afford to stay in a hotel. She's just a substitute teacher; she doesn't get paid a lot. And she doesn't have any money saved. Dad hasn't had a real job since we came to Canada. All he does is sit around and drink."

Inez was crying, so I passed her the paper napkins that I'd picked up at Tim Hortons.

I felt bone-headed asking her about a hotel. I mean, I guess a hotel must cost at least fifty bucks a night. I don't know why, but suddenly I was thinking about my $250 shoes, and wishing I had that money back so I could have given it to Inez. Even if it meant I had to wear my old shoes to the basketball camp.

Inez wiped her eyes. Then she kept talking.

"We're staying in this shelter, Slam. In the market. I guess Mom knew about it through one of her friends. It was scary coming down here in the middle of the night. We took a bus to Rideau Street, but then we had to walk through the market. All the bums sleeping on the streets and the drunk guys coming out of the clubs, whistling at us and making comments.

"We got a room at the shelter, but I couldn't get to sleep. Mom started telling me all this stuff about Dad. Stuff I didn't know, from a long time ago in Chile. How he was one of Pinochet's men. The secret police. How he lied about it to Immigration. Otherwise they never would have let him into Canada."

Pinochet's men. The guys who made my dad's brother "disappear." I never knew my uncle, but still, it sent a chill down my spine, thinking that someone could just "disappear" and never be heard from again. He couldn't do that to Inez, could he? Make her disappear so that no one would ever find her? Not here, I thought. Not in Canada. Still, I could see why Inez's mom didn't want to take any chances.

"I really want to play in the finals, Slam," Inez said. "But my mom won't let me go anywhere near the school. She doesn't want him to find us. She thinks he's so mad at us for leaving that he'll do something crazy. Especially after all that weird stuff that he did."

"The note," I said. "The dead fish."

"My mom kept tropical fish," Inez said. "She said it made her feel so peaceful to look at them. Why would he do that, Slam?"

"I don't know," I said.

I didn't tell her about her dad coming around the gym, looking for her. I mean, it was obvious now that the Billingsview Terrace guy was Mr. Ramirez. But why tell Inez about it? It would only make her more scared.

"You know what the stupid thing is, Slam?" Inez was crying again. "He was a really great dad when I was a little kid and we were living in Chile. He used to take me to the soccer games on the weekends. Let me sit on his knee and eat ice cream. He called me *mi corazón*."

Mi corazón—my heart.

Inez wiped her eyes and blew her nose

with what was left of the paper napkins. Then she got up, and I did too.

"I've got to go, Slam. I told my mom I was just going out to the drugstore."

I felt her body press against me, but the hug was so quick, I hadn't gotten over my surprise about it before she pulled away again.

"Tell the girls to win the finals for me," she said.

"I will," I said as I watched her walk out the door.

But I didn't want to think about the other girls playing the final game while Inez hid out in a shelter, afraid of her own dad. I wanted to see Inez back on the court, dribbling circles around the defense, sinking shots like the net was her own private property. I wanted her to lead the team to victory.

I just needed to think of a way to make it happen.

chapter sixteen

A few hours later, Ifrah and I were standing behind a concrete pillar outside the Billingsview Terrace apartment building. Don't get me wrong: I wasn't scared to take on Mr. Ramirez by myself. But I wanted a witness. When it came to witnesses, Ifrah was definitely the first-round draft pick. She'd brought her dad's digital video recorder, and her cell phone was set to call 911 on speed dial in case anything happened. Not that anything was going to happen. But try telling that to my stomach; it was jumping like a rebounder in a speed drill.

"You ready?" I said to Ifrah.

"Yeah," she said. "You sure you want to do this, Slam?"

"No sweat. I'm just going to talk to him."

"Hopefully," she said.

"Don't let him see you," I answered. I didn't even want to imagine what Inez's dad would do if he caught sight of some girl spying on him with a video camera.

It was a hot afternoon, with the sun beating down on the concrete landscape. The pillar we were standing behind held up a roof that jutted out over the building's front driveway. I didn't see anyone around, but I could hear the noise of an electric lawn-mower coming from somewhere around the corner. I stepped out from behind the pillar, crossed the driveway, went up a couple of stairs, opened the entrance door and stepped into the foyer.

Looking through the door to the lobby, I could see a woman in a headscarf with some shopping bags in her hands, waiting for the elevator. Other than that, the place looked deserted.

I scanned the panel and found the name Ramirez. My throat was so dry I could've chugged a whole bottle of Gatorade. Instead I swallowed hard and thought about what I was going to say when I saw Mr. Ramirez.

Sir, I'm a friend of your daughter's. I know you lied to get into Canada, and if you don't lay off her, I'm going to tell the police.

If he asked me how I knew about his past, I'd tell him my parents recognized him from Chile. There's no way I was going to get Inez into even more trouble.

But first I had to get Mr. Ramirez downstairs.

Ramirez. I stared at his name on the panel. Suddenly I felt like I was standing at the free-throw line before a critical shot— that moment of tension when everything depends on your next movement.

I jabbed my finger on the intercom button.

"Yeah?" A man's voice came over the speaker.

"Mr. Ramirez?" I tried to keep my voice steady. "FedEx delivery for you. Come down and sign for it please."

"Come up," the voice growled. A buzzer sounded to unlock the inner doors.

I was ready to take some heat from Inez's dad if it meant a chance to get her back on the court for the final game. But no way was I going up there alone to his apartment. There's a line between brave and stupid. For me that line was located at the inner door of the Billingsview Terrace apartment building.

"It's against regulations, sir. You'll have to come down," I said.

He let out a couple of curse words, and I thought, *if he's that upset over coming down for a FedEx delivery, what's he going to do when he finds out it's not a delivery after all?* But I put that thought out of my mind. It wasn't exactly helping me to focus on my mission.

"All right. I'm coming," he said.

I had planned to wait for him inside that little entrance foyer, but now the place was making me feel kind of boxed-in. Like one of those cages they use in ultimate fighting, where one guy comes out the champion and the other guy has to get his guts stitched back together before he can crawl out the escape hatch. I felt like I needed some open space, you know? So I stepped outside of the apartment building to wait at the top of the steps for Mr. Ramirez.

I looked around and saw Ifrah peeking out from behind the pillar with her video camera. I was starting to feel nervous about dragging her into this.

I looked back through the glass doors into the lobby. The woman with the headscarf was gone. Nothing moved for a little while. Then I saw the numbers above one of the elevators begin to light up. Eight, seven, six...G for ground floor. The doors opened, and out came Mr. Ramirez.

He looked like I'd dragged him away from his afternoon nap and he wasn't too happy about it. He was wearing work boots with the laces untied, a pair of gray sweatpants and a stained T-shirt. His hefty, hairy arms stuck out of the short sleeves. He had stubble all over his face, and his hair looked like it hadn't seen a comb since the night before—or longer. He opened the inner glass door, then the door that led outside, but he didn't come out of the building. He just leaned against the doorframe, holding the door half open and staring at me.

"Where's the package?" he said.

One fast sprint would have taken me right out of there. Across the driveway, past the pillar, down the hill, past the strip mall, out to the street and all the way home. Suddenly my legs were telling me that the best way to deal with this guy was to get out of town. But Ifrah was videotaping. No way was I going to let her see me turn tail. So I opened my mouth and hoped the words would come out the way I'd practiced them in my head.

"Sir, I'm a friend of your daughter, Inez."

"What the hell is this?" Mr. Ramirez took a step toward me.

"I know you lied to get into Canada..."

Wham. Pain exploded in my jaw. The back of my head cracked against the stairs. I tasted blood in my mouth as I tumbled backward. I tried to get to my hands and knees, but his boot hit me hard in the ribs. I sprawled to the sidewalk. I curled in a ball on my side and wrapped my arms around my head, bracing for the next blow. The boot hit me again in the ribs with a sickening crack. I screamed and tried to roll away. Then I heard a shout. "Stop it! Stop!"

Ifrah. I felt a stabbing pain as I lifted my head. Something blurred my vison— blood, or sweat—but I could see her coming out from behind the concrete pillar. Mr. Ramirez let out a yell and started toward her. I swung my feet around and caught him hard on the shin, just above the ankle. His body fell on mine, crushing me. Pain tore through my ribs. I struggled to get out from under him, stifled by his weight and the smell of sweat and alcohol. I got to my knees. His brawny arm hooked me around the neck. He pulled me backward, and I fought to pry his arm away. Suddenly a siren shrieked and tires screeched in the driveway. His arm let go, and I fell face-first, gasping, to the sidewalk.

Above me, voices shouted. There was a commotion of footsteps, flashing lights and the smell of car exhaust. I lay there, not moving, until I heard a voice close to me.

"Are you all right, son?" I looked up and saw the blue uniform of a police officer. I opened my mouth to say something, but only blood came out.

"Just hang on," the officer said. "The ambulance'll be here soon."

The next few minutes were a confusion of strange faces and voices. Two paramedics strapped me to a stretcher and wheeled me into the back of an ambulance. But before the ambulance doors swung closed, I saw one thing clearly: Mr. Ramirez, with his hands cuffed behind his back and a cop's hand on his shoulder, forcing him into the back seat of a police cruiser.

chapter seventeen

My face and my ribs were still throbbing when I went down to the courthouse on Monday morning for Mr. Ramirez's bail hearing. I'd spent Sunday afternoon at the hospital, the evening at the police station and half the night explaining things to my parents. With half my face covered in bruises and my ribs held together with elastic bandages, I didn't really feel like being out in public. But the cops said there was a good chance the judge would let Inez's dad out on bail unless they could prove he was a "danger to society."

I didn't know about society, but I knew for sure that if Mr. Ramirez got out of jail, Inez and her mom were going to go so far into hiding they'd probably bump into Osama bin Laden. And, obviously, Inez's mom was not going to let her play in the basketball finals on Thursday. So I wanted to sit right up front where the judge could see me. If my face didn't prove that Mr. Ramirez was a danger, I didn't know what would.

I got to the courtroom and slid onto the front-row bench next to Ifrah. I figured the cops must have got in touch with Inez and her mom, but I didn't see them anywhere. I was going to ask Ifrah about it when someone said, "All rise," and the judge walked in. The judge was a short woman in a black robe, with black hair done up in a bun and a strict look in her eye. After she climbed up to her chair behind a raised podium, an officer brought in Mr. Ramirez.

I hardly recognized the scruffy slob who had punched me out on Sunday. His face was clean-shaven, his hair was slicked back and he was wearing a blue suit jacket and a tie. A tie! That wasn't playing fair. How was he supposed to be a danger to society in a blue suit jacket and a tie?

"Your Honor." The prosecutor stood up. "We believe there is ample cause in this case to deny bail to the accused, Mr. Ramirez. The record shows that approximately three weeks ago, Mr. Ramirez was charged with assaulting his wife and daughter. He was released, pending trial, on condition that he keep the peace and have no further contact with the victims.

"Yet the evidence will show that while he was free on bail, Mr. Ramirez did contact his wife and daughter, with threats. And, following this, he savagely beat a young man, Salvador Amaro, who is seated here in court today."

The lawyer waved his hand toward me, and the judge turned her sharp eyes on my face. I tried to look like I was in excruciating pain. It wasn't hard—my jaw was throbbing like a subwoofer at a dance club.

"Your Honor, Mr. Ramirez stands before you today charged with assault and with breaching his bail conditions. Clearly, this man is not able to restrain his violent impulses and poses a danger if he is once again released on bail. The prosecution is therefore asking for Mr. Ramirez to be remanded in custody to await trial."

"Asking for what?" I whispered to Ifrah. I'd managed to follow most of the prosecutor's speech, but that last sentence sounded like gobbledygook.

"They want him kept in jail so he doesn't beat up on anyone else," Ifrah whispered.

You'd think if that's what he meant, he'd just *say* it. But I guess if he talked like normal people, no one would believe he'd been to law school.

The judge turned to the defense lawyer.

"And what is your position, Counsel?"

"Your Honor, my client has no criminal record. Furthermore, his actions in this case were purely in self-defense. We ask that he be set free until the duly appointed time of his trial."

I didn't get all of that either, but one word jumped out at me: *self-defense!* I just about leapt out of my seat when I heard that one. Ifrah grabbed my arm and pulled me down.

"You're not allowed to talk unless they call you to the witness box," she hissed.

It didn't make any sense. That lawyer was telling a bold-faced lie, and I wasn't even allowed to tell the judge the truth.

It was like in a game, when a player flops to draw the offensive foul. You know the guy's faking it, but if you try to tell the ref about it, you get in trouble for mouthing off. The judge looked like she'd kick me out of the courtroom if I talked out of turn. So I shut my mouth and plunked back on the bench beside Ifrah.

Pretty soon they set up a TV in the courtroom, and the prosecutor played Ifrah's videotape. Let me tell you, it is no fun watching a video of yourself getting beaten up. I wanted to shout *"Duck!"* when I saw Mr. Ramirez's fist coming toward me. Of course I didn't duck. A split second later I watched myself flying backward like a crash-test dummy in a car-safety commercial.

After the video, the prosecutor called the investigating officer to the stand. He told the judge that he had come on the scene to find Mr. Ramirez trying to strangle me, and that he had arrested Mr. Ramirez and charged him with assault.

Then it was the defense's turn to ask questions.

"Constable Willis," the defense lawyer said, "as we saw on the video that was shown earlier, it appears that Mr. Ramirez and the *alleged* victim had a brief conversation before the *alleged* assault took place. Do you know what was said during that conversation?"

The cop flicked through his notepad.

"I have a statement from the victim," he said.

That was the statement I'd given him Sunday evening.

"I'm not interested in what the *alleged* victim told you," said the defense lawyer. "I want to know if you heard that conversation yourself."

"No. I hadn't yet arrived on the scene."

"Then it's possible that the *alleged* victim made some kind of threats toward Mr. Ramirez? And that Mr. Ramirez was acting in self-defense?"

There he went again, talking about self-defense and the *alleged* victim. I wanted to tell him there was nothing *alleged* about a bruised jaw and two broken ribs.

"I don't know anything about any threats," said the cop. "The boy stated that he was there to speak to Mr. Ramirez about his daughter, Inez. Inez was his friend and he was concerned that her father might try to hurt her again."

"In other words," said the defense lawyer, "here we have a cocky young kid who wants to show off for a girl. So instead of calling the police if he fears for her safety, he decides to go around and intimidate her father."

Man, this defense lawyer was really starting to get on my nerves.

"I don't know about that," said Constable Willis.

"And do you know whether the young man was carrying a concealed weapon when he went to confront Mr. Ramirez? A gun or a knife?"

"I didn't check."

"Let me get this straight, Constable Willis. You arrived on the scene and you didn't even bother to check whether one of the people involved in the fight was armed?"

"The boy was in pretty rough shape," said the cop. "Our priority was to get him medical treatment."

"So you didn't even bother to check if he had a weapon," the defense lawyer insisted.

"If he did, he sure didn't know how to use it," said the cop.

"Thank goodness for that," said the defense lawyer. "No further questions." He sat down.

I don't know what was worse: the defense lawyer with all this stuff about concealed weapons, or the judge, who nodded like she was buying right into it. I mean, it really burns me that, just because you're a teenager, people think you've got a gun stuck in your jeans and ecstasy stuffed down your socks. But I stopped thinking about that when the prosecutor announced his next witness.

"Your Honor, I'd like to call Mrs. Juanita Ramirez to the stand."

A court official started to open the door at the back of the room, but the defense lawyer jumped up faster than a rebounder on a free throw.

"Objection, Your Honor. Mrs. Ramirez has nothing to do with the current assault charge against my client."

"Your Honor," the prosecutor argued, "I'm calling Mrs. Ramirez to testify about the charge of breaching bail conditions. Not about the assault."

The judge nodded.

"I'll allow the witness," she said. "But I expect you to keep your questions narrowly focused, Counsel."

The prosecutor agreed, and the next minute Inez's mom came into the courtroom. She was dressed in a skirt and a suit jacket with her black hair swept back from her face. Her eyes looked dark and heavy and sad. She stepped into the witness box and cast a look at Mr. Ramirez, sitting there in his respectable blue suit. Then she looked away in disgust.

"Mrs. Ramirez, can you tell the court where you are living at present?" the prosecutor began, after Inez's mom swore to tell the whole truth and nothing but the truth.

"At a women's shelter, Your Honor." Mrs. Ramirez looked directly at the judge, as if she was trying to ignore everyone else in the courtroom. Trying to pretend that her whole private life wasn't getting put out there for everyone to see.

"And how long have you been living there?"

"About three weeks."

"Since your husband assaulted you?"

"Allegedly, Your Honor!" The defense counsel sprang to his feet.

"Allegedly," the prosecutor corrected himself.

Mrs. Ramirez nodded. "Yes."

"Mrs. Ramirez, has your husband contacted you since that night?" the prosecutor continued.

"Not directly, no."

"Indirectly?"

"Yes. He sent two threatening messages to my daughter's school. The school where I'm a substitute teacher and coach the girls' basketball team."

"And what did you do as a result of these messages?"

"I took my daughter out of school, Your Honor. And I stopped coaching the team."

"And why did you do that, Mrs. Ramirez?"

"Because I was afraid of him, Your Honor."

"Afraid of your husband?"

"Yes."

"No further questions."

The judge nodded, and I thought we were in the clear. No way was a female judge going to let this guy out on bail. Then the defense lawyer got up for the cross-examination.

"Mrs. Ramirez, these messages that arrived at the school. What exactly did they say?"

Mrs. Ramirez tightened her lips.

"They were...vague."

"They didn't actually threaten you with harm then?"

"You have to understand my husband," said Mrs. Ramirez. She didn't look at Mr. Ramirez, but the judge did, sitting there in his dapper blue suit. Man, what a hypocrite.

"Mrs. Ramirez," the defense lawyer continued, "how do you know these messages came from your husband? Were they signed?"

"My husband was in the Chilean secret police," Mrs. Ramirez burst out. "He knows better than to sign a threat. Even when he's drunk."

"So they weren't signed." The defense lawyer stuck to his point.

"Of course not." Mrs. Ramirez sounded disgusted.

"But you believed they were from him."

"Yes, I believed it. Of course they were from him."

"And, believing this—however untrue—you sent young Salvador Amaro to confront your husband, to threaten him, didn't you?"

Man, this defense lawyer sure knew how to spin a story. Mrs. Ramirez looked away from him and spoke directly to the judge.

"Your Honor, I would never send a boy to confront a grown man. Especially not a violent man, like my husband."

"Perhaps your daughter did then," the defense lawyer shot back. "No further questions, Your Honor."

Mrs. Ramirez looked like she had a lot more to say about her jerk of a husband, but the court official escorted her out of the witness box. She shot a look at Mr. Ramirez as she passed him, but he didn't look at her.

He just sat there in his blue suit with his shoulders thrown back and his eyes straight ahead, like a soldier under inspection.

The court was silent as she walked out, and the door closed behind her.

"What's going to happen?" I whispered to Ifrah.

She gave a little shrug. "Up to the judge."

The judge was studying some papers as the two lawyers made their short, final speeches. The more I looked at the judge, the more she reminded me of the kind of teacher who fails kids for grammar mistakes and gives out detentions for whispering in class. I got the feeling she wanted to send someone to the principal's office, but she wasn't sure if it should be me or Mr. Ramirez.

Finally she cleared her throat and spoke.

"Whether Mr. Ramirez acted in self defense is, obviously, not for me to decide. That's a question for the trial. The question before me today is whether he poses an unacceptable risk if he is released on bail.

"I must say, I am reluctant to send a man to jail who has not been found guilty of a crime. On the other hand, Mr. Ramirez was released on bail once before, and—regardless of the circumstances—he has failed in his promise keep the peace."

The judge turned to the defense lawyer.

"You've asked for Mr. Ramirez to be released. Does he have anyone who can act as a surety?"

I nudged Ifrah.

"What's a surety?"

"Someone to make sure he doesn't get into trouble," she whispered.

"Your Honor, my client is a recent immigrant from Chile. He has no close friends here."

"Family?"

"Only his wife and daughter."

"Yes. I see." The judge picked up her gavel.

"I'm going to order Mr. Ramirez remanded in custody on the grounds that he poses a danger to society. Counsel, let's set a trial date for as soon as possible."

She banged her gavel once, and that was it. The guard took Mr. Ramirez's elbow and led him down to the jail cells. Then the lawyers shuffled some papers, and a guy accused of shoplifting was brought into the prisoner's dock.

I wanted to give Ifrah a high five, but she shook her head. I guess if you're serious about becoming an RCMP officer, you don't go around high-fiving people in a courtroom.

Outside in the hallway we looked around for Mrs. Ramirez, but we couldn't find her. Inez wasn't there either.

"You think they'll be back for the finals?" Ifrah said.

"They're coming back," I said. "No way Inez is going to miss that game."

chapter eighteen

There's something about a championship trophy that gets me juiced.

I don't care if it's an Olympic gold medal or a silver spray-painted Little League cup, a trophy's the thing that says: we are the best. And once your name's engraved on it, it's there forever.

The National Capital Secondary School Athletic Association Girls' Basketball trophy was sitting on the scorekeeper's table when I got to the gym at 3:45 on Thursday.

The sight of it made the ache in my ribs disappear. It was like instant painkiller. I knew that cup was ours to win.

Inez was stretching her calf muscles against a wall. She had her dark hair up in a ponytail, and there was no trace of a bruise left on her cheek. Not like me: the whole left side of my face looked like an eggplant.

"Hey, *cómo estás?*" I said.

"*Muy bien*," she said. That means "really good." Then she gave me a smile, like *I* was the one making her feel really good.

You know that feeling when you're at the top of a perfect jump shot? You're hanging in the air, and you've just let go of the ball. You can feel it flying in a perfect arc toward the basket, and you know it's heading for nothing but net. The feeling never lasts for more than a second, but when it happens, you know you've hit life on the sweet spot. That's how I felt when Inez smiled at me and said *muy bien*—really good.

Inez grabbed a basketball that was lying next to her on the floor and went to practice some shots. I went over to Mrs. Ramirez to get the starting lineup to hand in to the ref.

Mrs. Ramirez looked pretty tense. She didn't say anything about my face or about the bail hearing. I didn't know if she was grateful that I helped get her husband locked up, or ticked off at me for messing around in her family life. There wasn't time to talk about it, because the ref blew his whistle and the girls gathered around for one last huddle. Then the buzzer sounded to start the game.

Ifrah won the jump, and Inez brought the ball up the court. The Glebe defender was hanging onto her like a buddy who wants to borrow five bucks. That didn't faze Inez. She put the ball through her legs and around her back. It was like she was telling everyone on the court: *This ball is mine. Just try to take it away from me.*

Inez reached the top of the key. Brenda cut down low and set a screen for Ifrah. Ifrah popped out into the center of the key and called for the ball. A sharp pass. Turn, jump shot, two points. It took me a second to realize what was happening.

"Hey," I said to Mrs. Ramirez, "you're running my offense."

"It's a good offense, Salvador," she said. "You did a good job."

The way she said that last bit made me think that maybe she wasn't just talking about basketball. Maybe she meant I did a good job by standing up to Mr. Ramirez. But like I said, there was no time to have a conversation about it. We had to focus on the game. And the game was too close for comfort.

The teams battled back and forth for every point. But the biggest battle was between Brenda and Glebe's tough girl, number 20. They were like attack dogs with a personal grudge. I mean, aggressive is good, but you've got to be smart aggressive. Dumb aggressive gets you fouled out—and that's exactly what happened to Brenda. Fouled out on a charging call, with the score tied at thirty and four seconds left in the first half.

By the time the buzzer sounded and we crowded into the change room, the girls were soaked in sweat and so pumped they were bouncing off the lockers. I mean, rattling the metal. Glebe had missed the free throw, so the score remained tied. Now it was time to step it up.

"Okay girls, we're going to lay on a full-court press," Mrs. Ramirez said. The idea was to force some turnarounds and pull into the lead early in the second half. She gave them some reminders about setting a trap for the point guard. Then she turned to Maddy.

"You're in for Brenda," she said.

You could tell Mrs. Ramirez wasn't too happy about the situation. Maddy was our best six-man, but she was supposed to be a point guard. She didn't know Brenda's position. Anisa was supposed to be Brenda's sub, but you couldn't put in Anisa against that number 20 Glebe girl. She'd get eaten alive.

If we hadn't had Inez as our point guard, I think we would have been toast in the second half. But Inez was in the Zone. Her defender couldn't have pried the ball away from her with a crowbar. She zipped off passes left and right, or sometimes she just deked the defender out and drove for the basket. Ifrah was grabbing the rebounds like the ball was her long-lost baby brother. So with two minutes left in the game, the score was Glebe 61; Brookfield 60.

Inez was bringing the ball down the court. Her defender was trying to force her to the sideline, but Inez crossed the ball behind her back and cut to the inside. Down near the key, the other girls were setting up. The defender was expecting Inez to pass or drive, but just before she reached the three-point line, Inez picked up the ball and took a shot.

It was a beautiful thing to watch that ball arc toward the net. It soared over the defenders and dropped with a *swoosh*, like money in the bank. Three points. I didn't even know Inez could shoot like that. But suddenly we were on top: 63–61.

With just over a minute left to play, Ifrah intercepted Glebe's inbounding pass under the basket. While the defenders crowded in to block the easy shot, Ifrah passed it out to Inez, who was waiting all alone at the three-point line. Another shot: 66–61.

Our bench was going wild. I was going wild, even though my jaw felt like a tenderized lamb chop. Glebe brought the ball down the court, but our girls stuck to them tight. The Glebe point guard took a shot, but it rebounded off the rim. Glebe kept possession, but couldn't get another shot away. They passed it back out to set up the play again. Finally another shot, and this time a basket. Score: 66–63 for us and only twenty seconds left to play.

Ifrah took the ball at the baseline. Inez outran her defender and caught the inbounding pass. Glebe's only chance was to force a turnaround in our end. Two girls moved in to double-team Inez, but that left Maddy open. Inez snuck a bounce-pass through one defender's legs. Maddy caught it and started down the court. A defender scrambled to cover Maddy. Inez broke free of the second defender and called for the ball. She took the pass from Maddy and burned toward the centerline. Way down in the frontcourt, Ifrah, undefended, called for the ball with five seconds left on the clock. Inez heaved her the baseball pass. Ifrah caught it and turned to the basket. She dribbled in for the layup, banked the ball against the glass and...the final buzzer ended the game.

Did Ifrah score? I couldn't tell you. All I know is suddenly a horde of girls rushed onto the court, screaming. Then Inez was up on their shoulders, hoisting the trophy above her head.

A few minutes later, the Carleton University scout appeared at our bench to offer Inez a scholarship to summer training camp.

I didn't get a chance to talk to Inez until later on, when we were standing in line together at Cinnamon's. The team had basically taken over the place. There were duffel bags lying around everywhere and girls overflowing from their regular corner booth. The silver trophy sat on a table in the middle of it all. They had the barista dude grinding and foaming in overdrive. You couldn't hear anyone talk unless you were standing right next to them. Which was kind of a good thing, actually, because I was standing right next to Inez.

"Man, I didn't know you could shoot like that," I said.

"There was a basketball court in the basement of that place where we were staying. I've been practicing my three-point shots for the past two weeks."

"Cool," I said. I smiled at her, and Inez smiled back.

"Thanks, Slam," she said. "I mean, for standing up to my dad like that."

"Yeah, well, what else could I do?" I shrugged. "We needed you back for the finals."

Inez put her hand in her pocket and pulled out a scrap of paper. It was a bit crumpled and ragged around the edges, like she'd torn it out of a notebook. She pressed it into my hand.

"My mom and I got a new apartment," she said. I looked down at the piece of paper. There was an address and phone number written on it.

I don't know what I would have done next—kissed her, I guess—because suddenly it felt like the two of us were trapped inside some kind of a magnetic force field. But then the barista dude said, "Hey, what can I get you guys?" and I realized we were standing at the front of the line.

"Small coffee, please," said Inez.

"Make that two." I reached into my pocket, pulled out a five-dollar bill and laid it on the counter. Then I added, "Together."

chapter nineteen

My face was still bruised when I showed up at Ottawa U at six o'clock Friday morning to catch the bus to the development camp in Toronto. Coach Donovan took one look at me and scowled.

"What happened to you, Amaro? You get into a fight?"

"Yes, sir," I said.

"I oughta leave you here."

He stared at me, and I knew what he was thinking: what kind of a jerk gets into a fight just before an important tournament? The kind of jerk he shouldn't have picked for his team. Finally he hiiked his thumb toward the bus.

"Get on," he said. Then he turned away like he was too disgusted to look at me.

I wished there was some way I could explain. But what was I going to do? Tell Coach Donovan all about Inez and her dad and how he gave me a beating when I tried to stand up for her? That was her private life. I didn't have any right to go spilling it around. And besides, what if Coach Donovan didn't believe me? What if he thought I was just making up a story to try and make myself look like a hero?

I wished I could talk to Mike, but he hadn't made the final cut. So I told myself to suck it up. The important thing was, I was going to Toronto.

The development camp was at York University. Ten teams of the best guys from around the province duking it out through two days of skills and drills on Friday and Saturday, followed by a two-day tournament on Sunday and Monday. At the end of the tournament, the head coach from Toronto would choose the best twelve players to represent Ontario at the Canadian Nationals in August. The stakes were high and these guys were good. Really good.

I played my hardest in the skills and drills, but I could tell I was only in the middle of the pack. My ribs were wrapped in elastic bandages, and pain shot through them every time I'd bend or twist. By the time I got back to my dorm room on Saturday evening, it hurt just to breathe.

You want a recipe for *loud*? Take 120 teenage basketball players and put them in a college dorm. That is a recipe for *loud*. Normally, I wouldn't mind. I'd be right in there with the rest of the guys, eating pizza and playing cards and watching videos. But that Saturday night, I was lying on my bed with my face throbbing and an ice pack on my ribs, thinking: *how am I going to make the provincial team in this kind of shape?*

On Sunday morning after breakfast, Coach Donovan called the Ottawa guys together in one of the locker rooms and handed out the red T-shirts we'd be wearing for the tournament. Then he picked his starting lineup.

He barely even looked at me.

"Yousof, you're on as point guard."

It wasn't fair. I knew I was better than that Yousof kid. And how was I supposed to impress that head coach from Toronto if I didn't get a chance to play in the tournament? I opened my mouth to say something, but Coach Donovan shot me a look, and I clamped it shut. What was I going to do? Complain? Argue? That just showed disrespect for the coach. And dissing the coach— that would get me benched for good.

It wasn't until the last game on Monday that I got to play. It was a game against Toronto Central, the strongest team in the tournament. The stands were packed, and the head coach was sitting front and center, scouting out the guys before making his final picks for the provincial team.

Ottawa didn't look too hot. By the third quarter we were trailing 42–68. That's when

Coach Donovan called Yousof off the court and sent me in.

Maybe it's something about growing up next to the CN tower, but these Toronto guys were *tall*. And strong. Like steel girders.

The forward passed the ball in to me, and I started taking it up the court. The guy guarding me was one of those tall, lanky kids with arms you could wrap around a California Redwood. I thought I'd test him out by pulling a few dribbling moves. I put the ball between my legs and spun to the right—the kid was there. Around the back and deke left—the kid was there. At the top of the key, I finally managed to fake him out just long enough to get a good pass away to the shooting guard, who was breaking for the basket. Two points—but we had to work for them.

When Toronto came back at us on offense, that point guard had lightning in his fingers. He matched all my dribbling moves and added some of his own. I was keeping up, but just barely. Not enough to stand out from the pack.

I needed a chance to show that Toronto head coach something special.

And then I got it.

It was midway through the fourth quarter. Our center caught a rebound in the backcourt and passed it out to me for a fast break. I'd just crossed the centerline when the guy defending me somehow tripped over his own feet. I was in the clear, heading for the basket. A shout went up from the Ottawa bench, but it seemed to come from a million miles away. All that existed in the gym for me was the basket, gleaming at the far end of the court, and the pounding—of my feet, of the ball, of my heart—as I drove toward it.

I was in the Zone. I hit the key at top speed. This was my chance. I'd practiced the move a million times. My signature move. My right foot hit the paint. I sent the ball down after it, bouncing hard against the floor. My left foot pounded down as the ball came back up into my hands. I planted my right foot and drove up with my left knee. Airborne, I passed the ball under my left knee, around my back, into my right hand, lifted it high. Pain shot through my ribs, bone grinding against broken bone, but I drove through the pain, drove the ball up to the basket and then higher still, above the rim, and brought it down through the hoop, smashing it in with both hands. Slam dunk!

Cheers erupted from the stands. My feet hit the ground and it was like I'd broken through the sound barrier. The shouting and stamping hit me like a wave. I looked over at the Ottawa bench and saw something sweeter than all the cheers from my teammates. It was the look on Coach Donovan's face. Impressed. I knew if there was one thing that would get me on the provincial team, that was it. My one moment of hope.

The spaghetti banquet that evening was held in the York University dining hall, a huge room with rows of solid wood tables. All the coaches sat in their jackets and ties at a head table on a platform at one end.

Each team sat together. At the Ottawa table, the guys were still talking about my slam dunk. *Awesome move, Slam. Sweet.* But I wondered if one awesome move was enough to qualify me for the provincial team. At the end of the supper, the head coach stood up and called for everyone's attention.

"Boys, there's a lot of talent in this room tonight. You've shown it to us over the past four days. Everyone's played hard, and narrowing it down to the best twelve players has been tough. Some of you will make the cut, and most of you won't. But I want you all to know we appreciate the effort you've put in, coming to camp this weekend. Now, without further ado, here are the players chosen for the Ontario Under 17 team."

He cleared his throat. "Mohammed Khan..."

A guy let out a whoop and jumped from his seat in one corner of the dining hall. There was a round of cheers and high fives from his buddies, while the rest of us felt our hearts sinking one notch further into the pits of our stomachs. The head coach kept reading. "Marc Tessier..."

Number three, number four, number five...number ten, number eleven. Finally number twelve.

No more names on the list.

No Salvador Amaro.

The waiters came out with some trays of desserts, but I didn't have the heart to eat anything. As soon as I could get away, I slunk up to my room to start packing my duffel bag for the bus home.

It wasn't fair. I was a way better player than the Salvador Amaro the head coach had seen this weekend. If only I hadn't been so bruised and battered...But the bruising came from standing up for Inez. And if I hadn't stood up for her, she never would've had the chance to play in the finals, to win the high school championship. She'd still be hiding out, afraid of her dad.

I knew I'd done the right thing. But weren't you supposed to be rewarded for doing the right thing? What was my reward? Three broken ribs and a long bus ride home to Ottawa. Some reward.

I was just zipping up my duffel bag when Coach Donovan knocked on my door.

"Hey, Coach. Just about ready," I said, trying to smile.

"You've got grit, Amaro," he said. "You put in a good effort this weekend."

"Thanks, Coach," I said. I guessed he was making the rounds of the dorm rooms, trying to cheer up all the losers. I wished I could explain things to him. I knew it wouldn't change anything about making the provincial team, but at least it might give him a better opinion of me. I wanted him to know I wasn't a jerk. If I was bruised and beaten-up, it was for a reason. A reason that was even more important than playing basketball in the Canadian Nationals.

"You play for a club, Amaro?" Coach Donovan asked.

"No, sir. Just on my high school team. And I help coach a girls' team." The team that had gotten me into this mess. And I'd thought the assistant-coach gig would help me make the provincial team. What a joke.

"I coach a team. The Ottawa Lumberjacks," Mr. Donovan said. "Practices are Tuesday and Thursday evenings at St. Pat's high school. We could use a good point guard."

I didn't know if I'd heard him right. This was the coach who'd been riding me for the past three weeks. The guy who, I thought, hated my guts.

"Seriously?" I said.

"You're planning on trying out for the provincial team next year, aren't you?" he said.

"Yeah, for sure. I mean, definitely, sir."

"Good. Then we've got a year to get you ready for it."

He handed me a business card with his name and phone number and *Ottawa Lumberjacks* printed on it.

"See you Tuesday, Amaro." He turned and walked off down the hallway.

I stood there staring at his business card like he'd just handed me a hundred-dollar bill. No, it was better than a hundred-dollar bill. A hundred-dollar bill, you get it and you spend it. This was a chance to improve myself. To improve my game. If anyone could whip me into shape, it was Coach Donovan. I put my hand into my pocket to tuck the card away for safekeeping. As I did, I felt another piece of paper in there. I pulled it out. It was the paper with Inez's phone number on it.

A date with Inez. A spot on Coach Donovan's team. Maybe those were my rewards. Not the kind of reward I'd expected. Not like a medal for bravery or a championship cup. But the kind of reward that's an opportunity for the future.

I tucked Inez's phone number back into my pocket and slung my duffel bag over my shoulder. Soon I'd be on the bus, heading back to Ottawa. But somehow, it wouldn't be the same old hometown I'd left. It would feel like a new place, with new opportunities.

Maybe next year, I'd be back here in Toronto listening to the head coach call out my name in the banquet hall for the Ontario team.

Maybe I'd be kissing Inez to celebrate.

Acknowledgments

I would like to thank Deb McAskin for reading the manuscript with an eye to the technicalities of basketball. Any remaining mistakes in the text are mine, not hers. Similarly, my thanks go out to Chabine Tucker for taking the time to discuss Basketball Ontario's Under 17 Program with me and for allowing me to attend a tryout.

For help on the long and uncertain road toward publication, I am grateful to the members of my writing group and to my mother, who has shared my love of writing and literature for as long as I can remember (What larks, my dear, what larks!) Thanks also to Sarah Harvey at Orca Book Publishers for making me feel like I'd won the lottery when she called to offer me a book contract.

Finally, and with all of my heart, I would like to thank my husband Mark for supporting my writing, even when it seemed futile, and for taking extra shifts with our newborn to allow me to finish this novel.

Kate Jaimet is a reporter for the *Ottawa Citizen* and a former high school basketball player. The mother of a baby and a kindergartner, she lives, works and battles sleep deprivation in Ottawa, Ontario.